I0443530

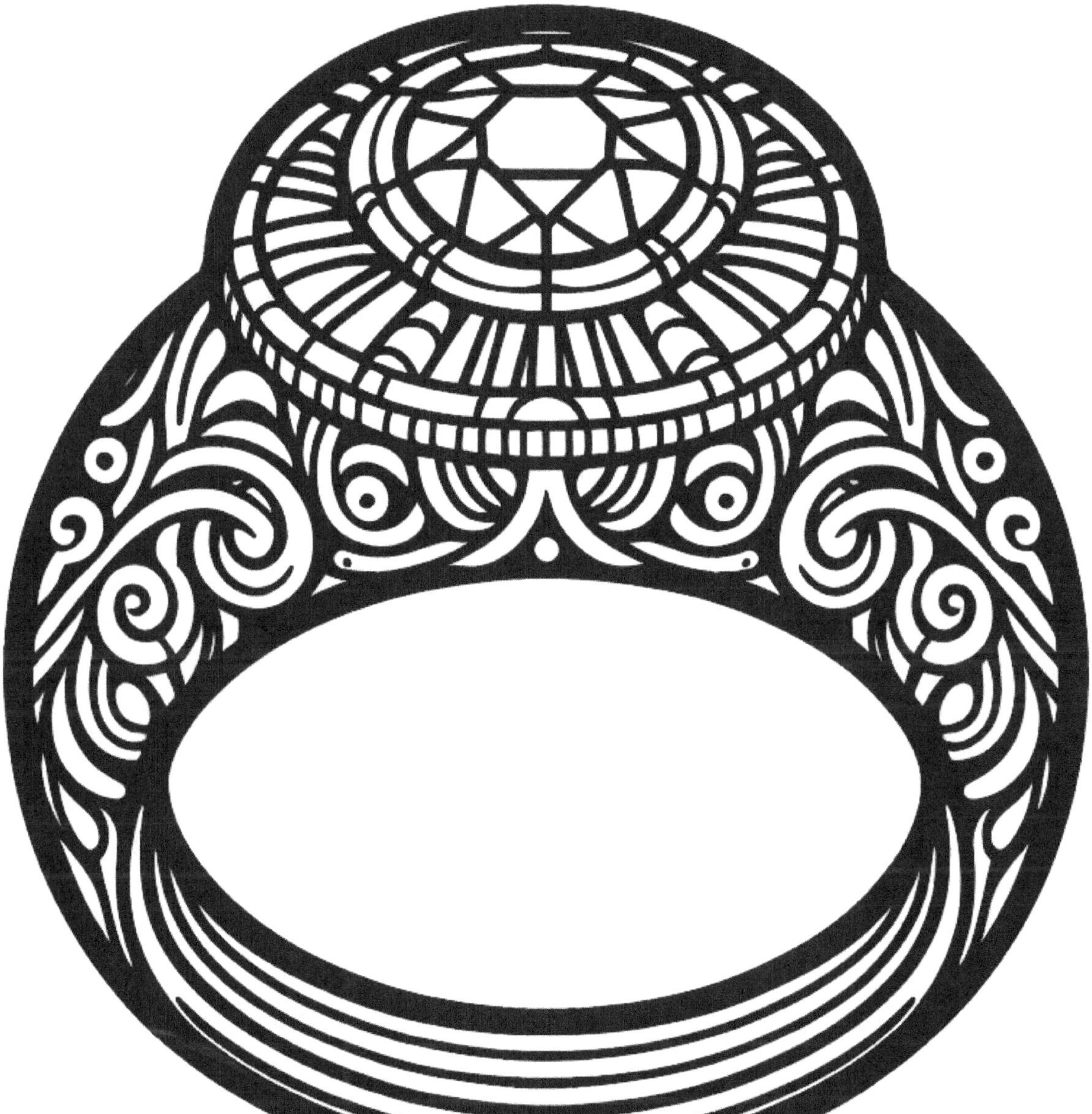

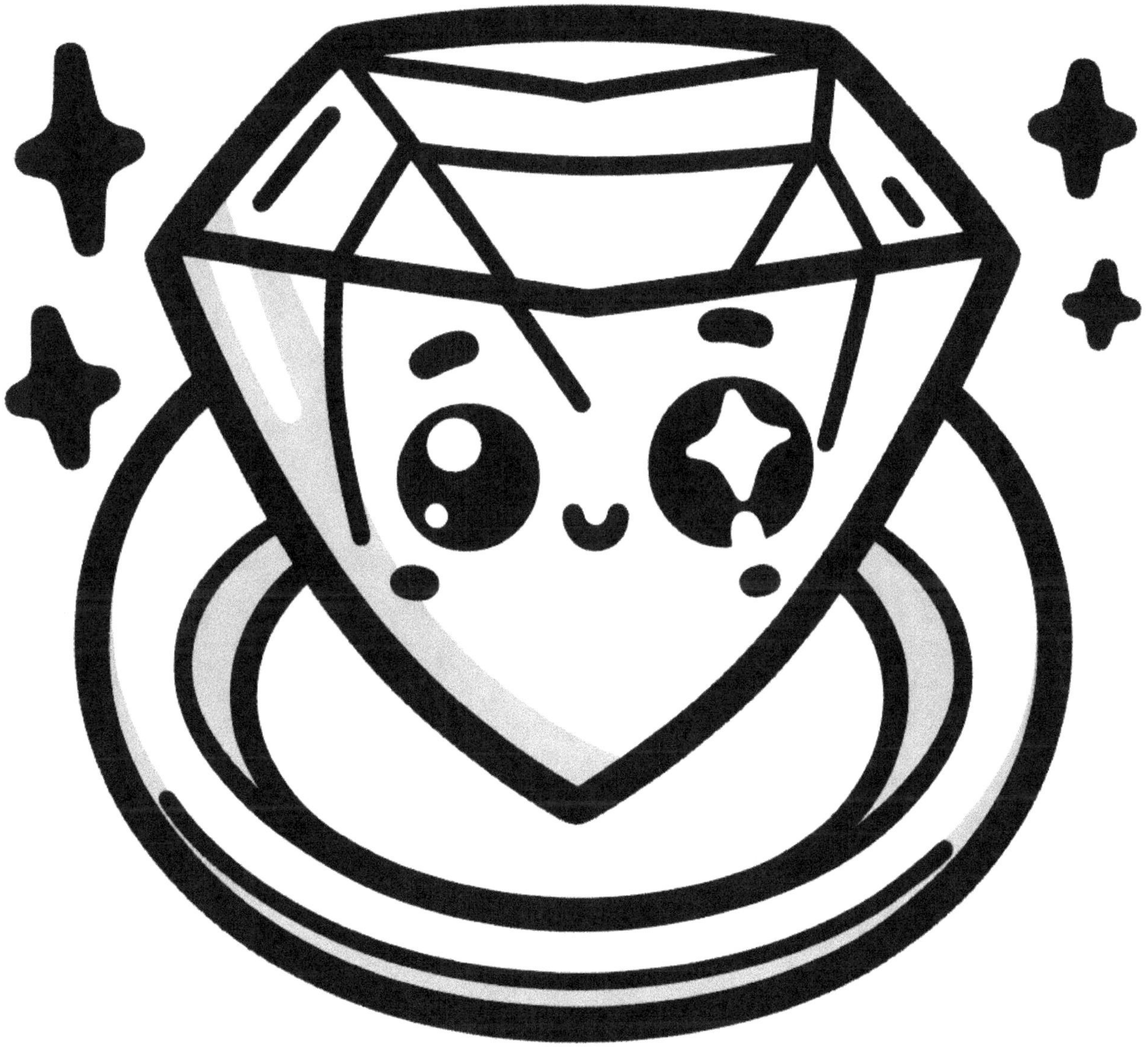

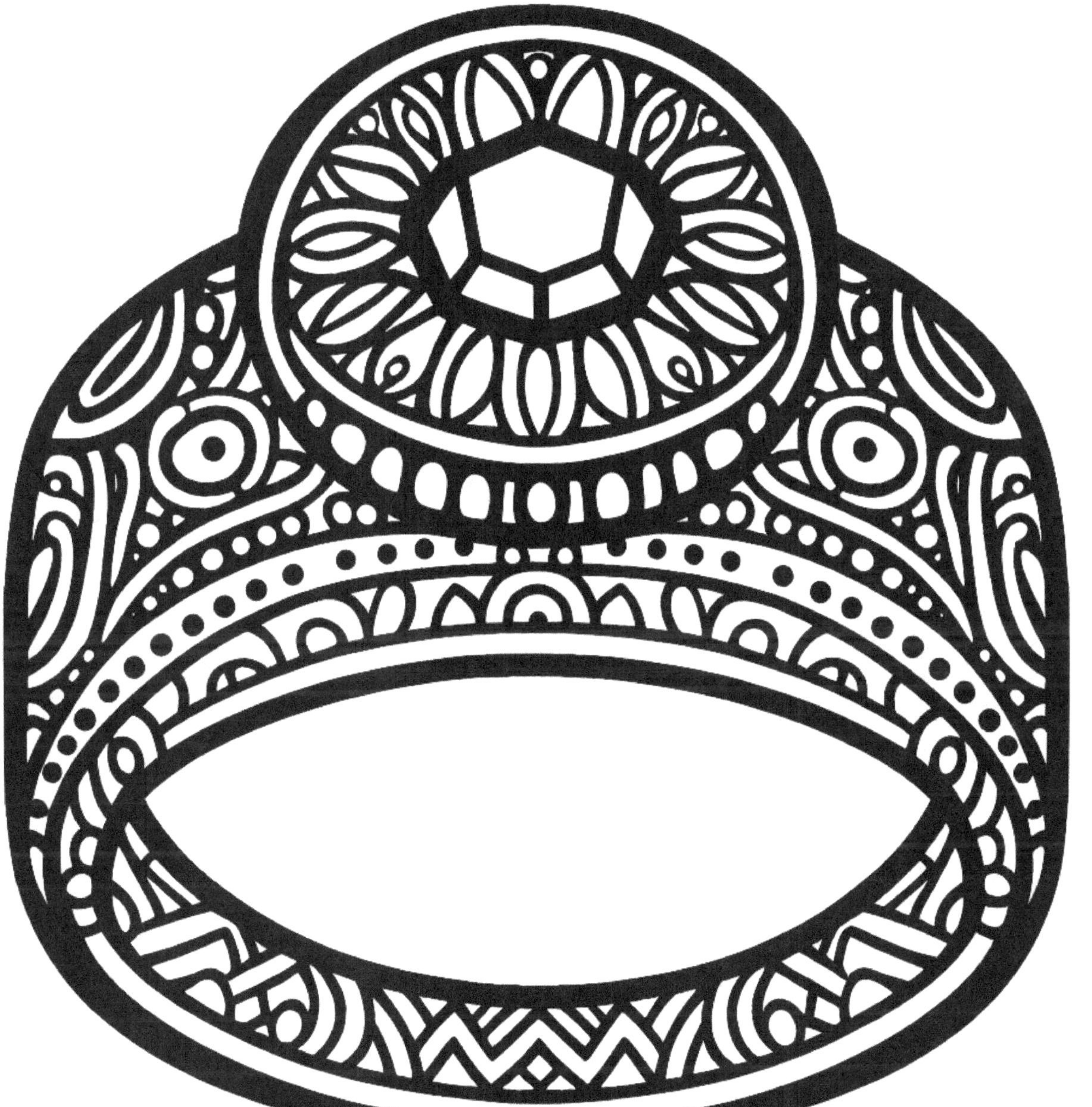

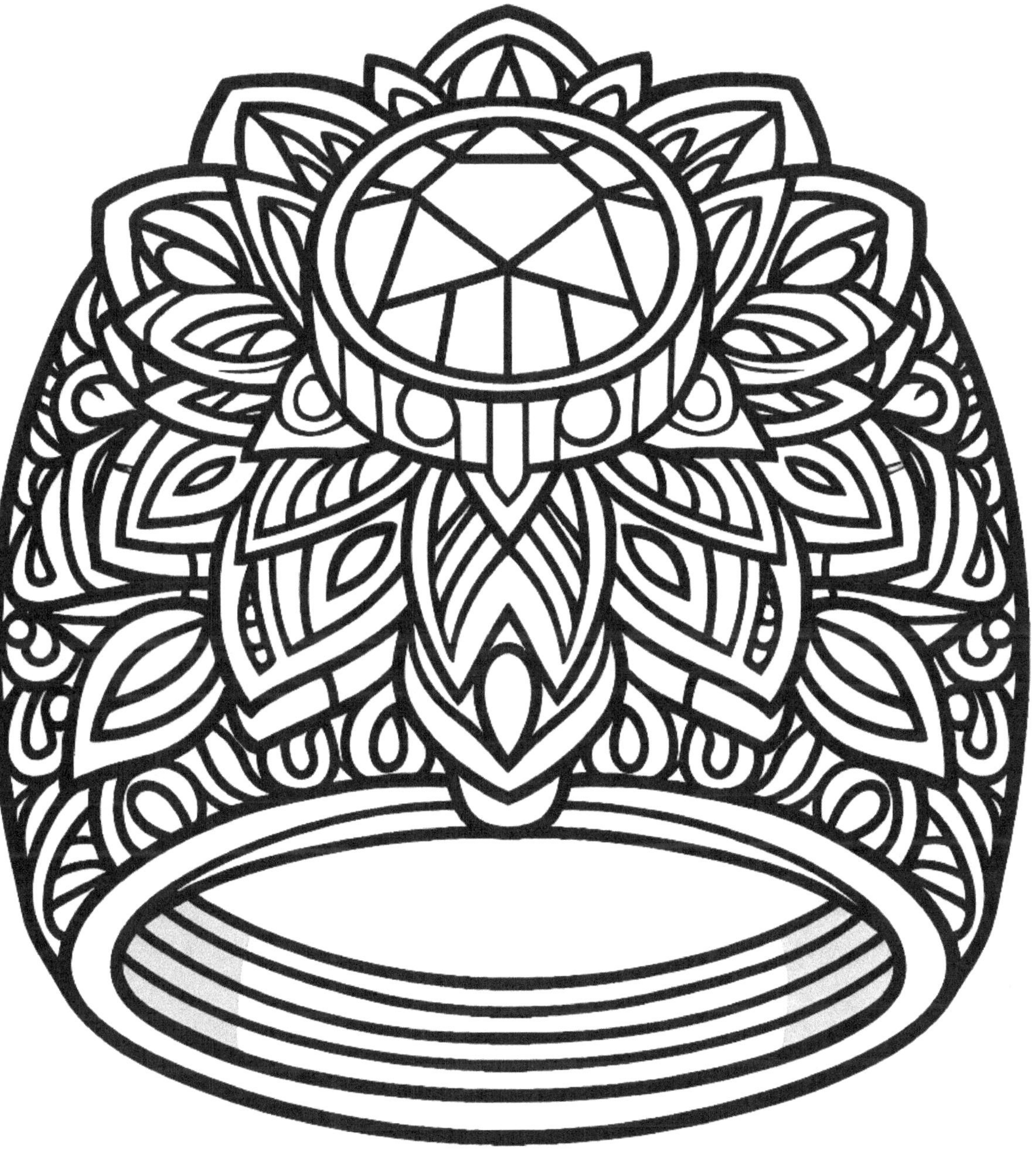

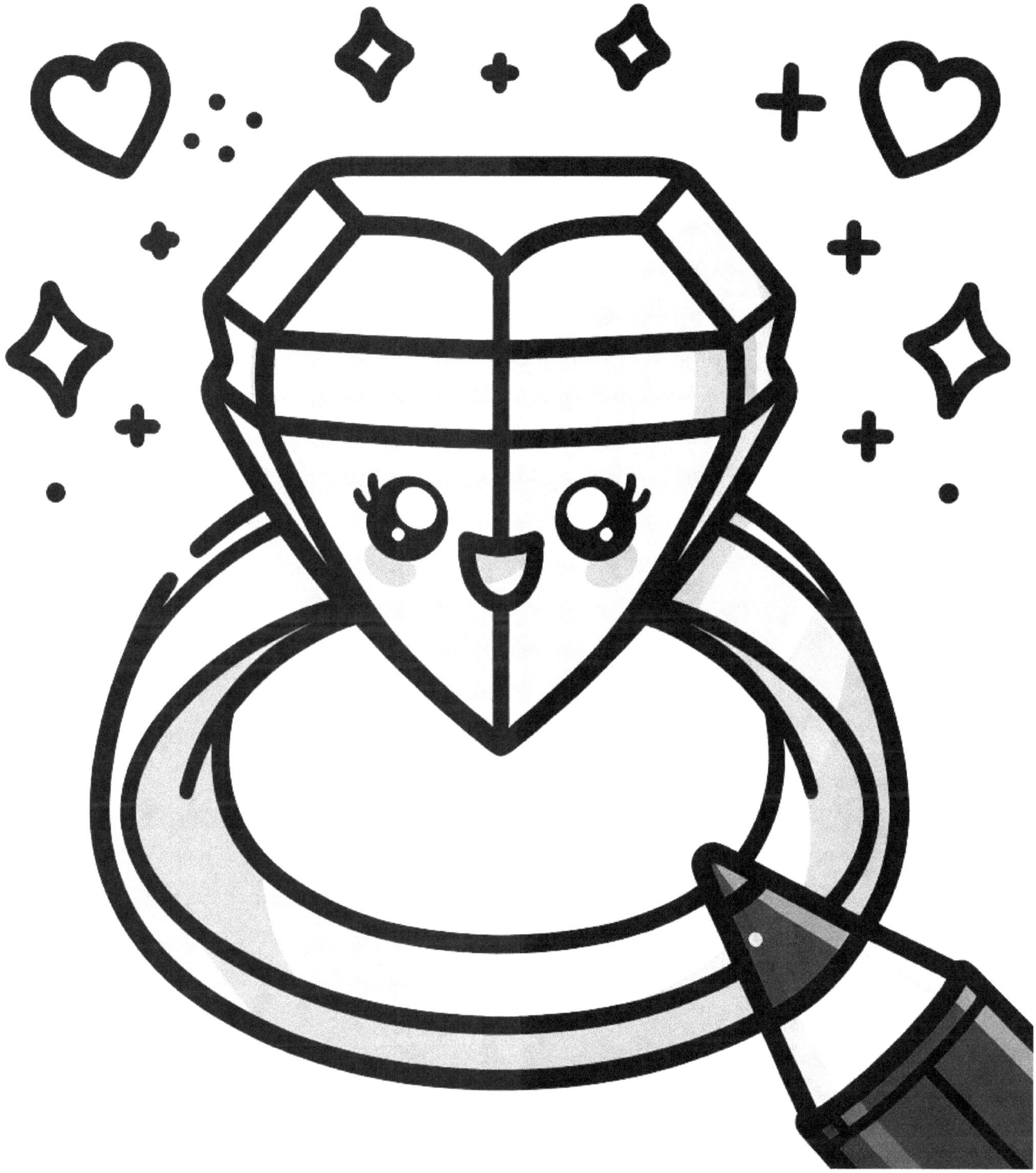

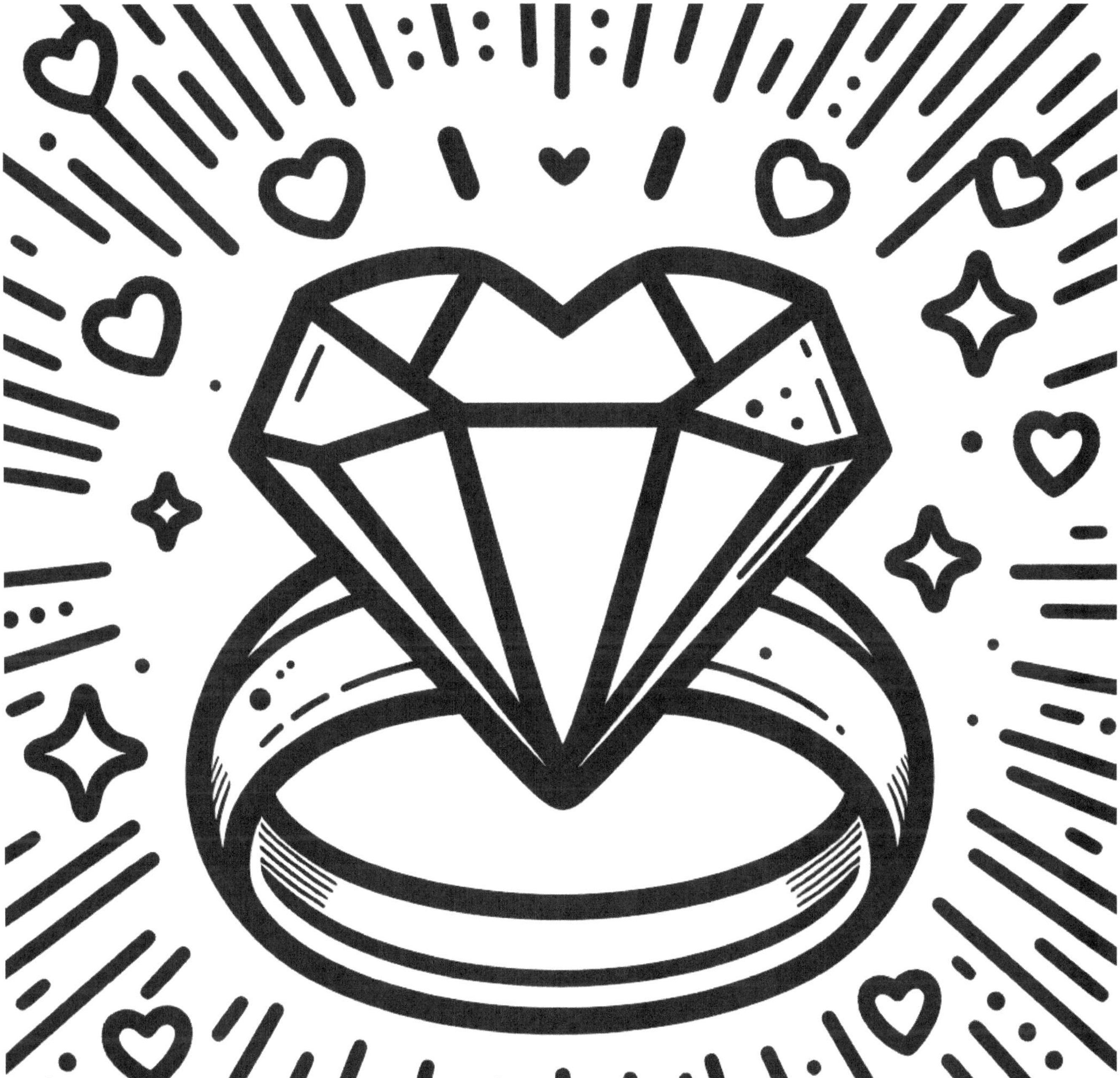

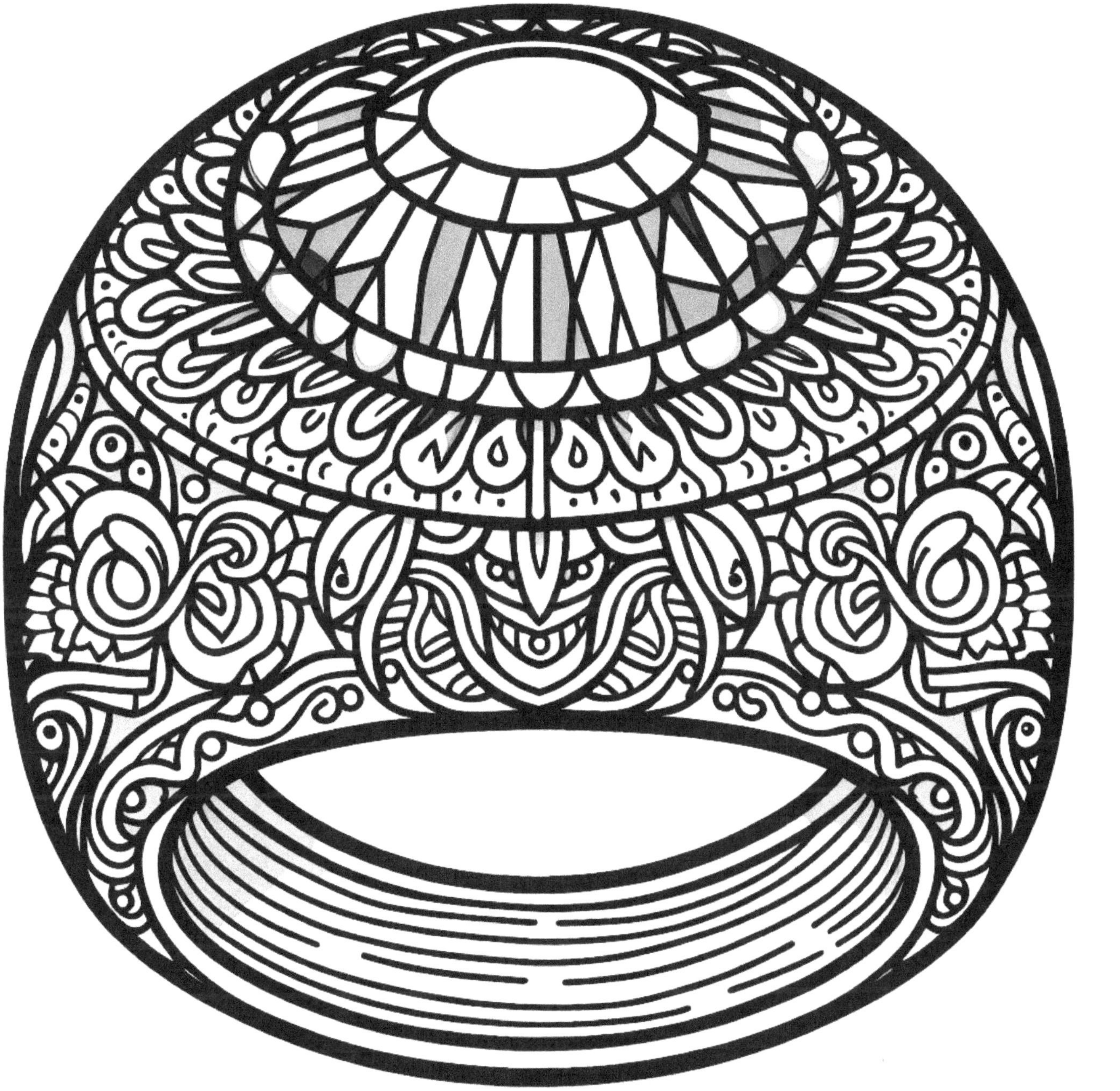

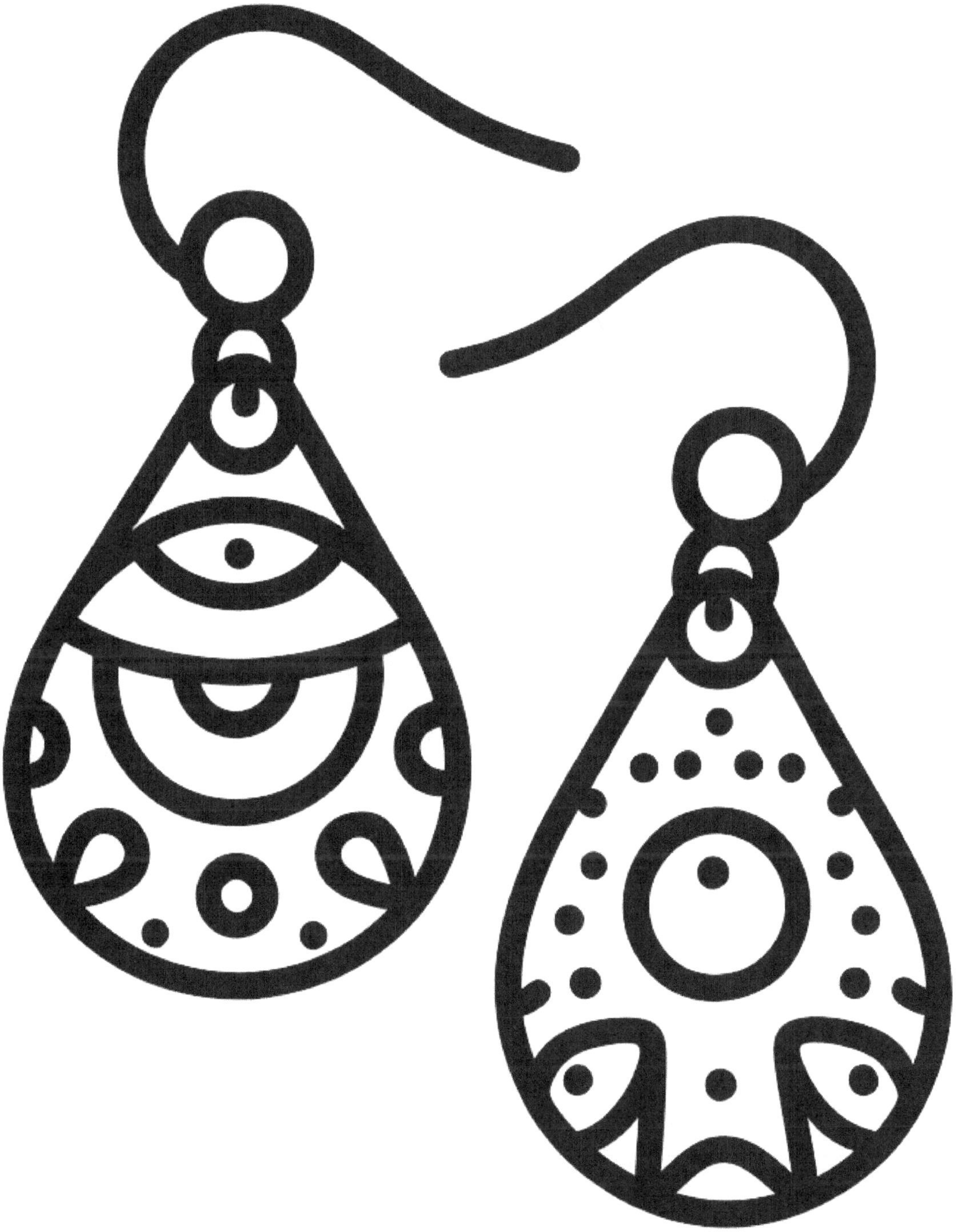

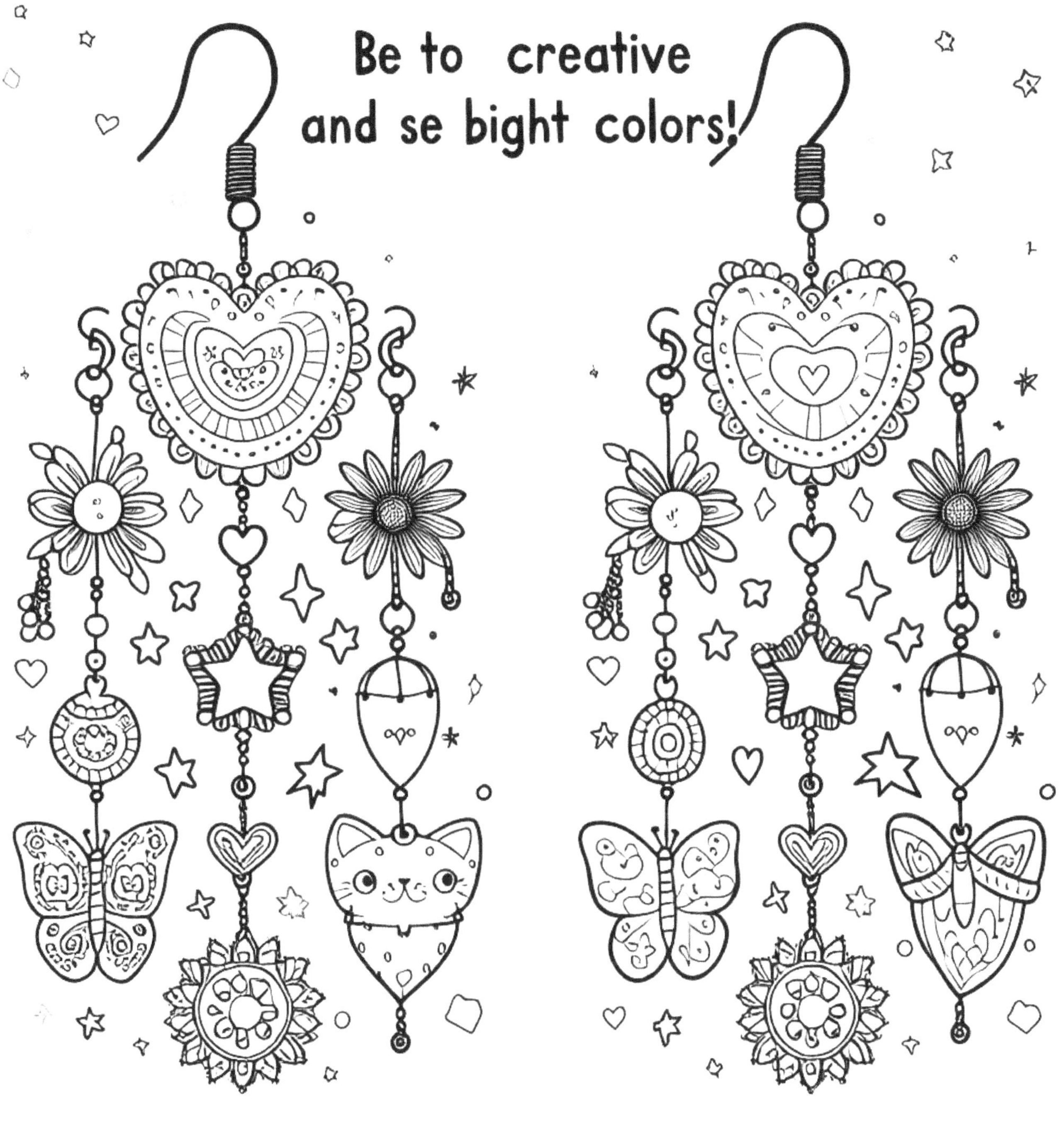
Be to creative
and se bight colors!

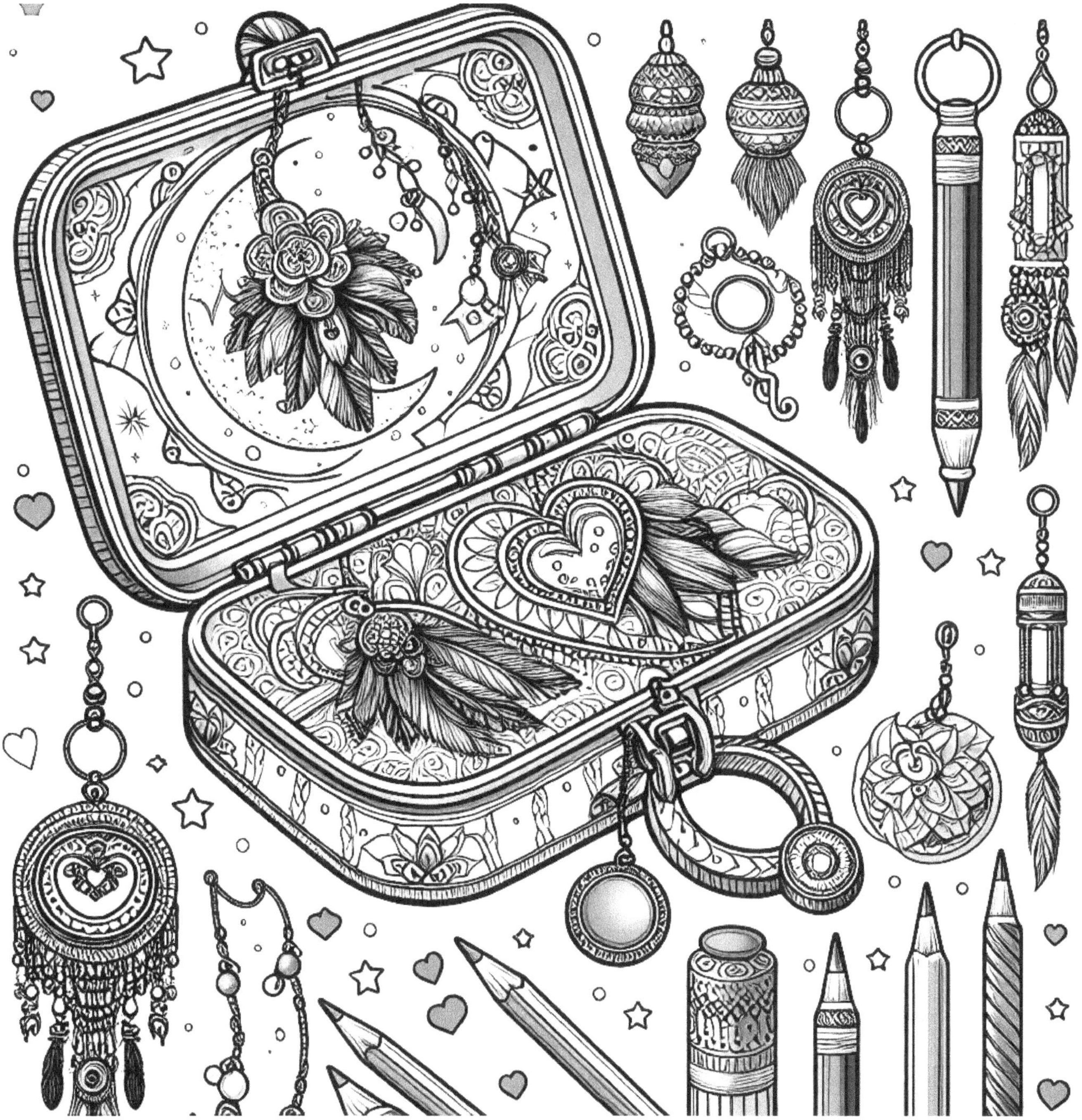

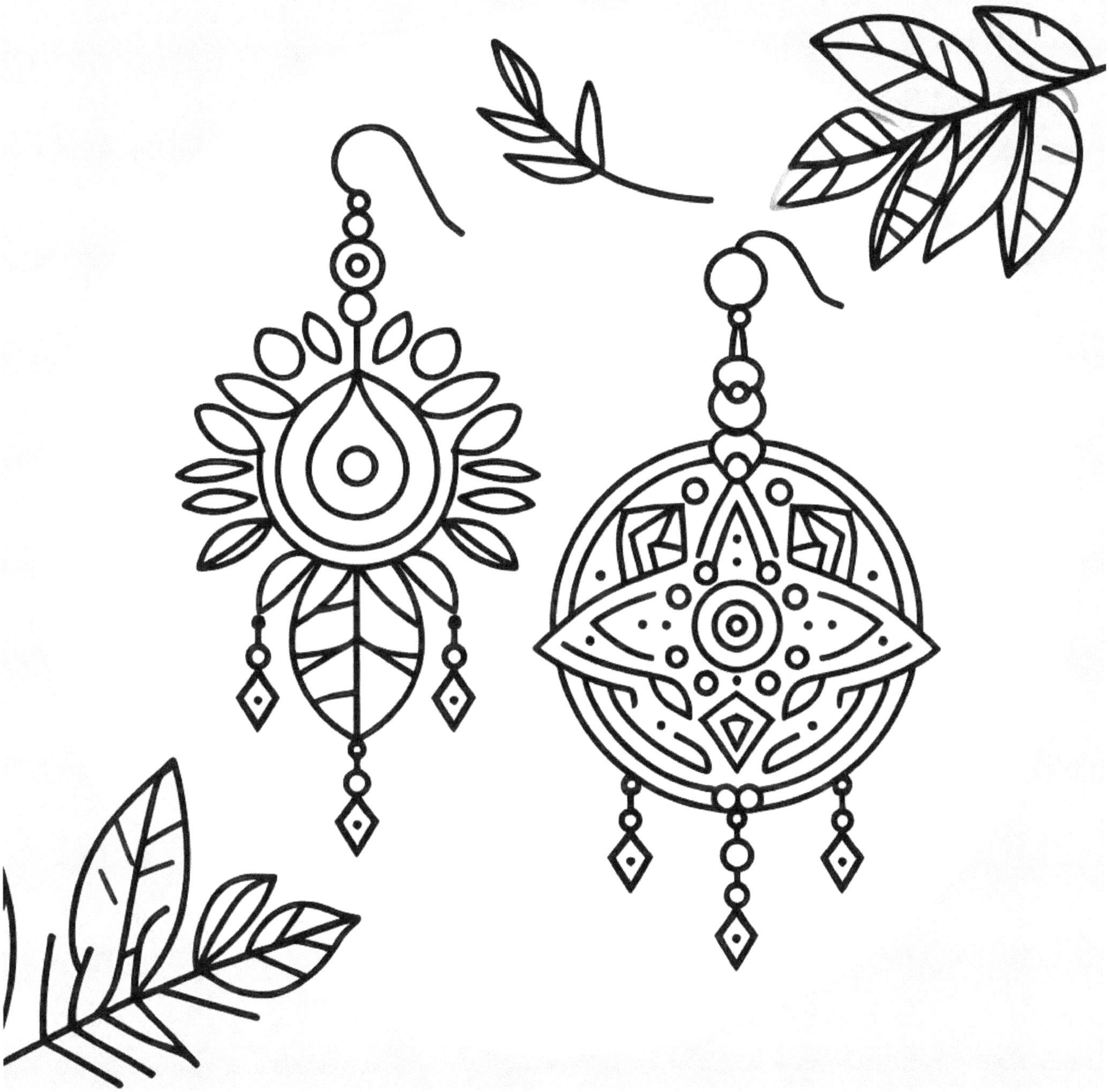

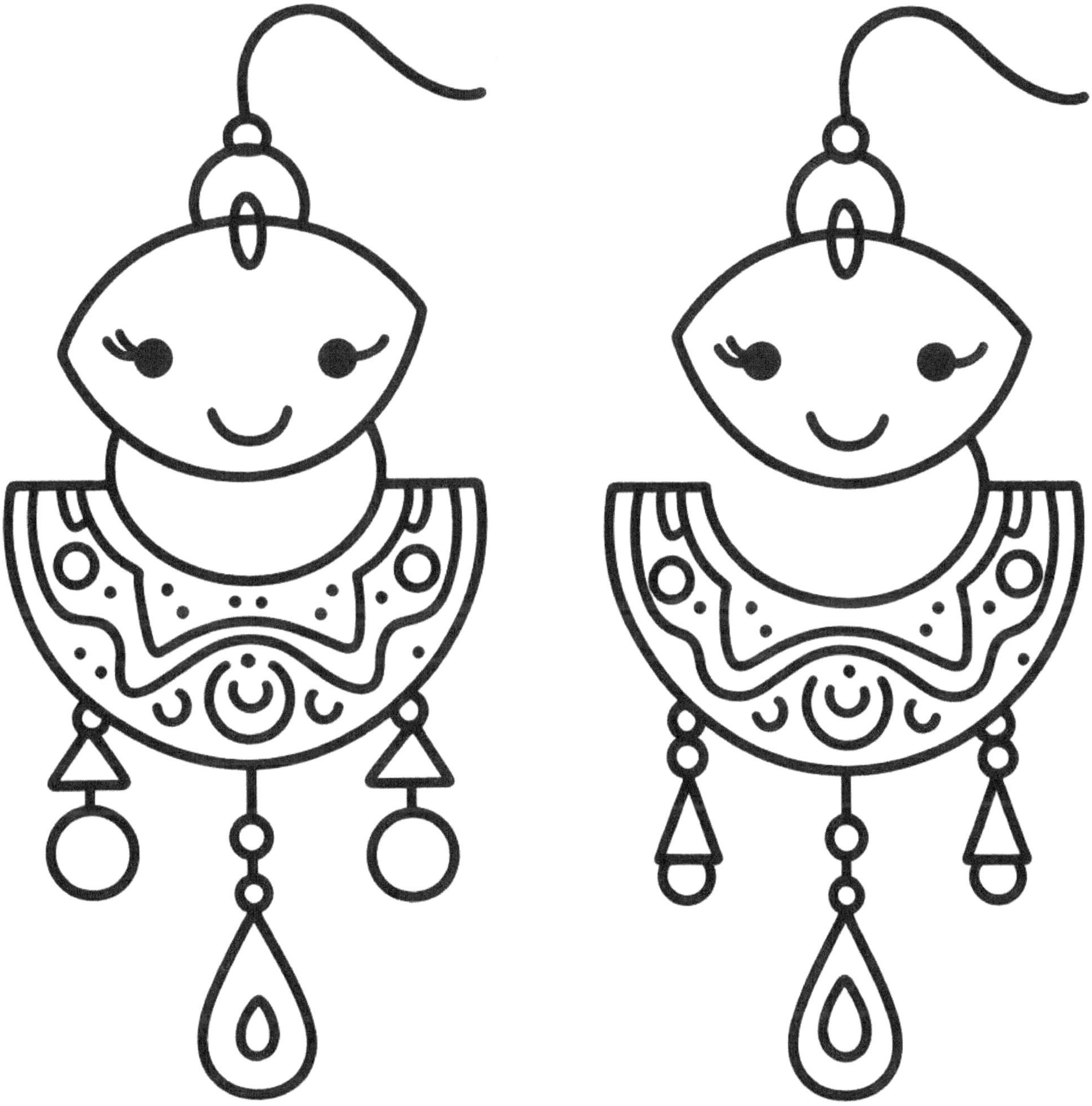

Be your brigIt colors!

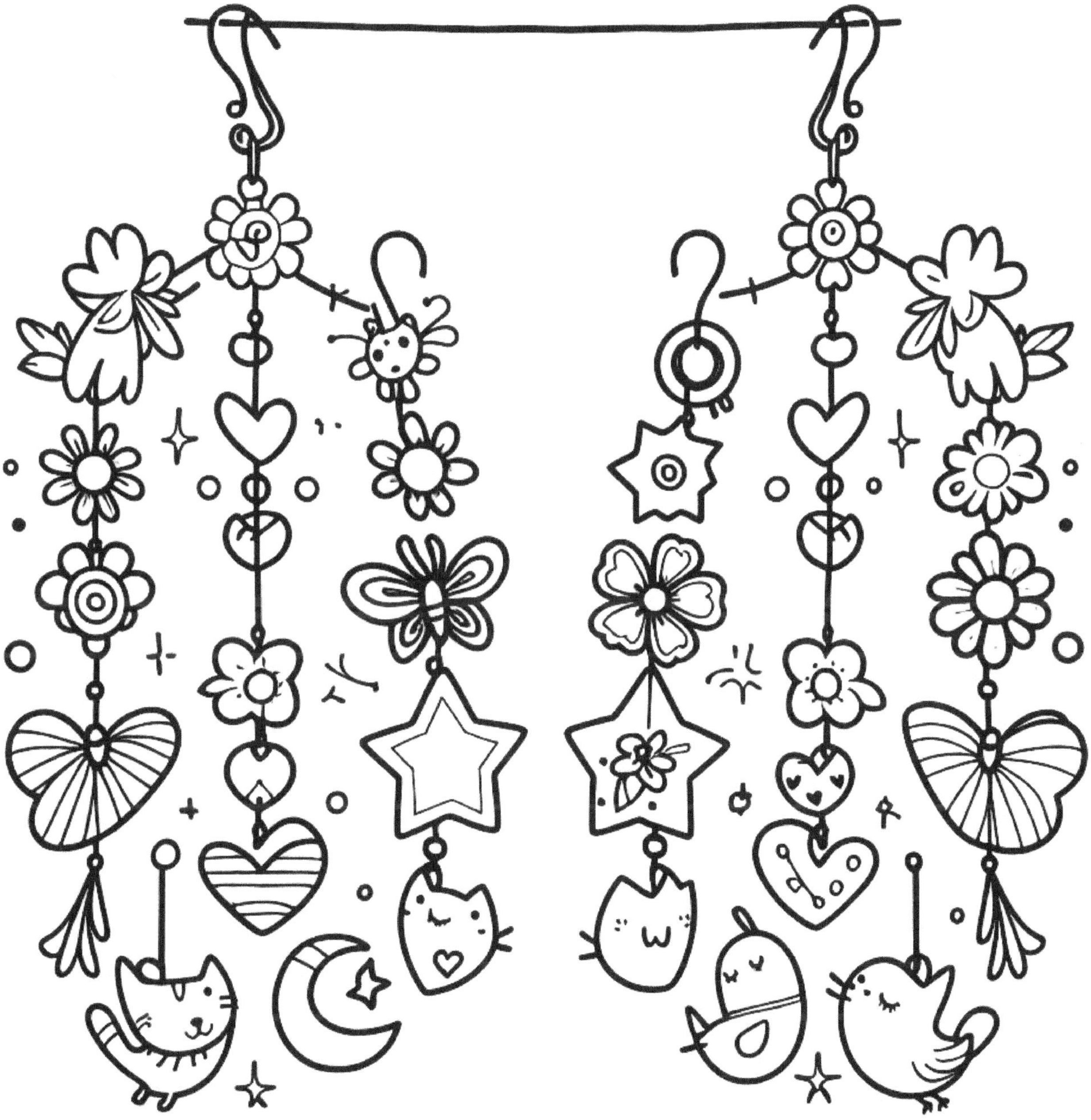

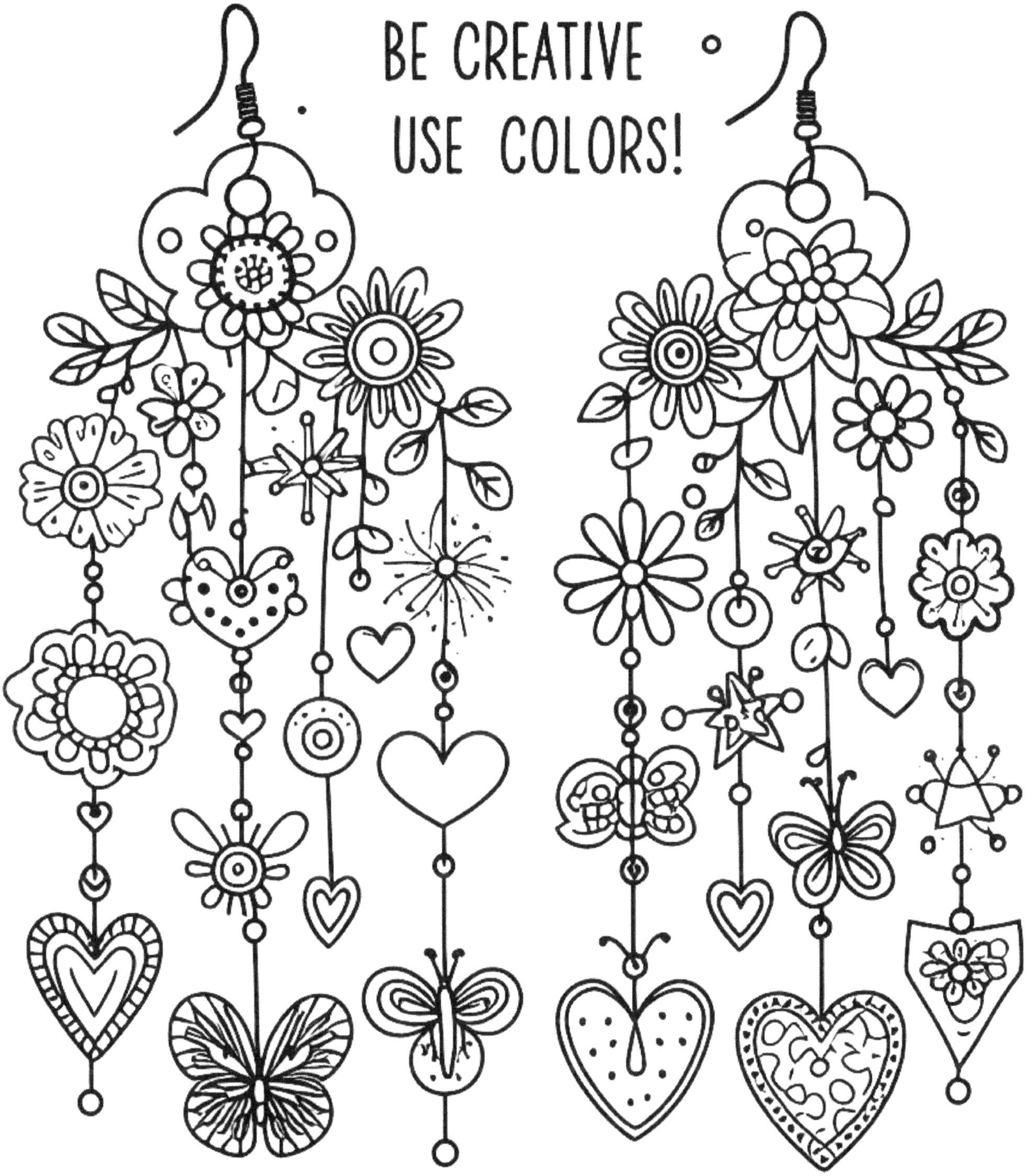
BE CREATIVE
USE COLORS!

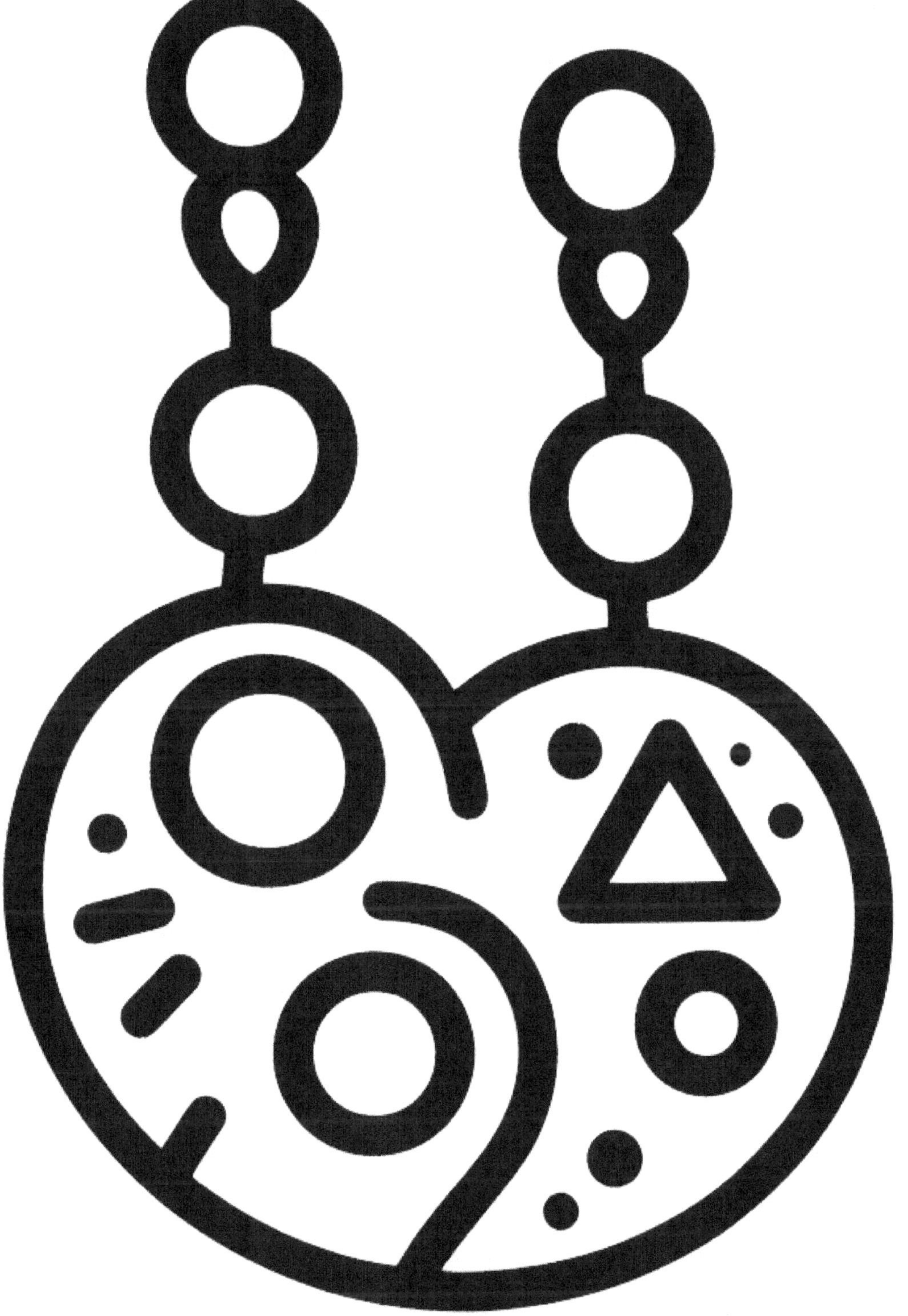

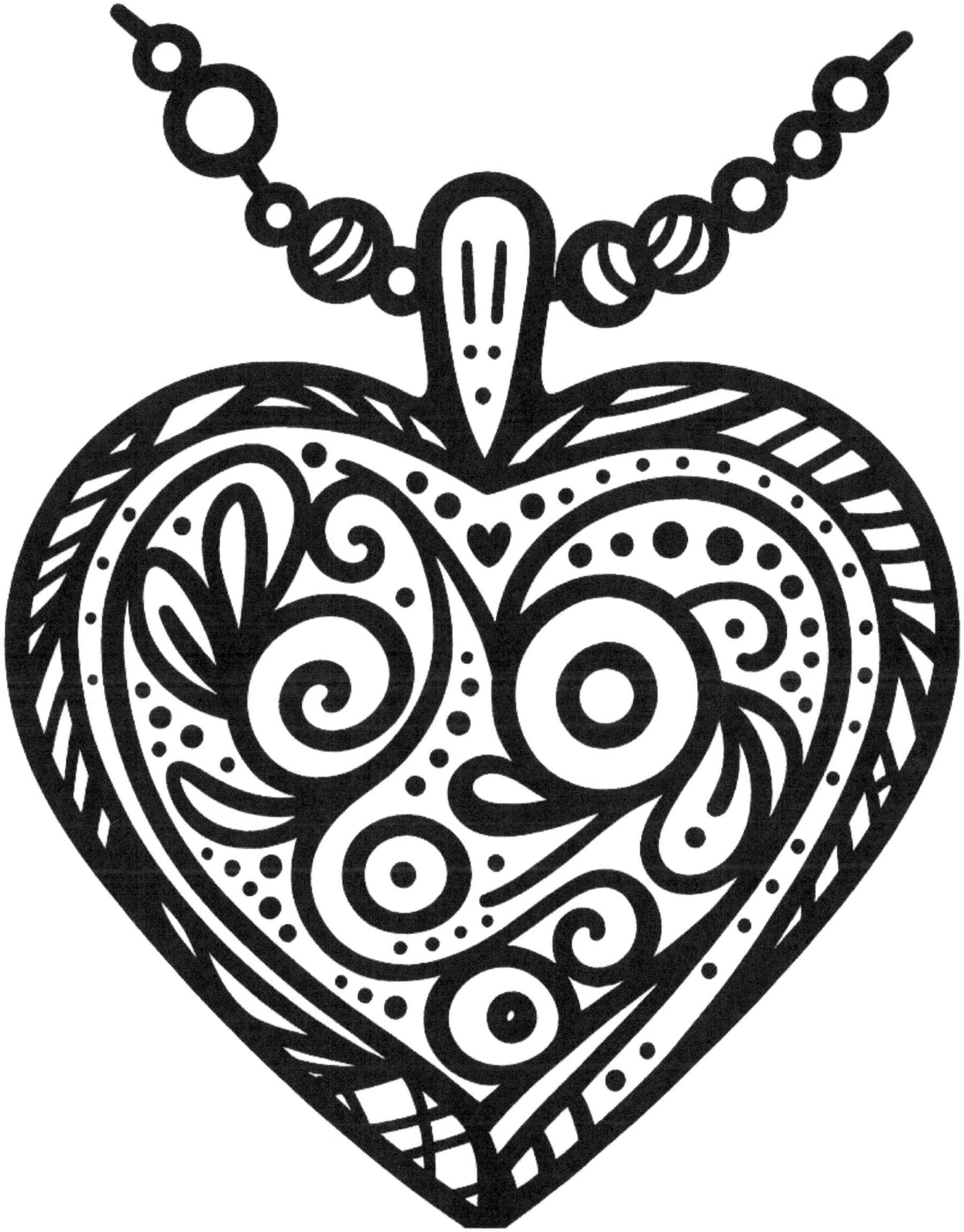

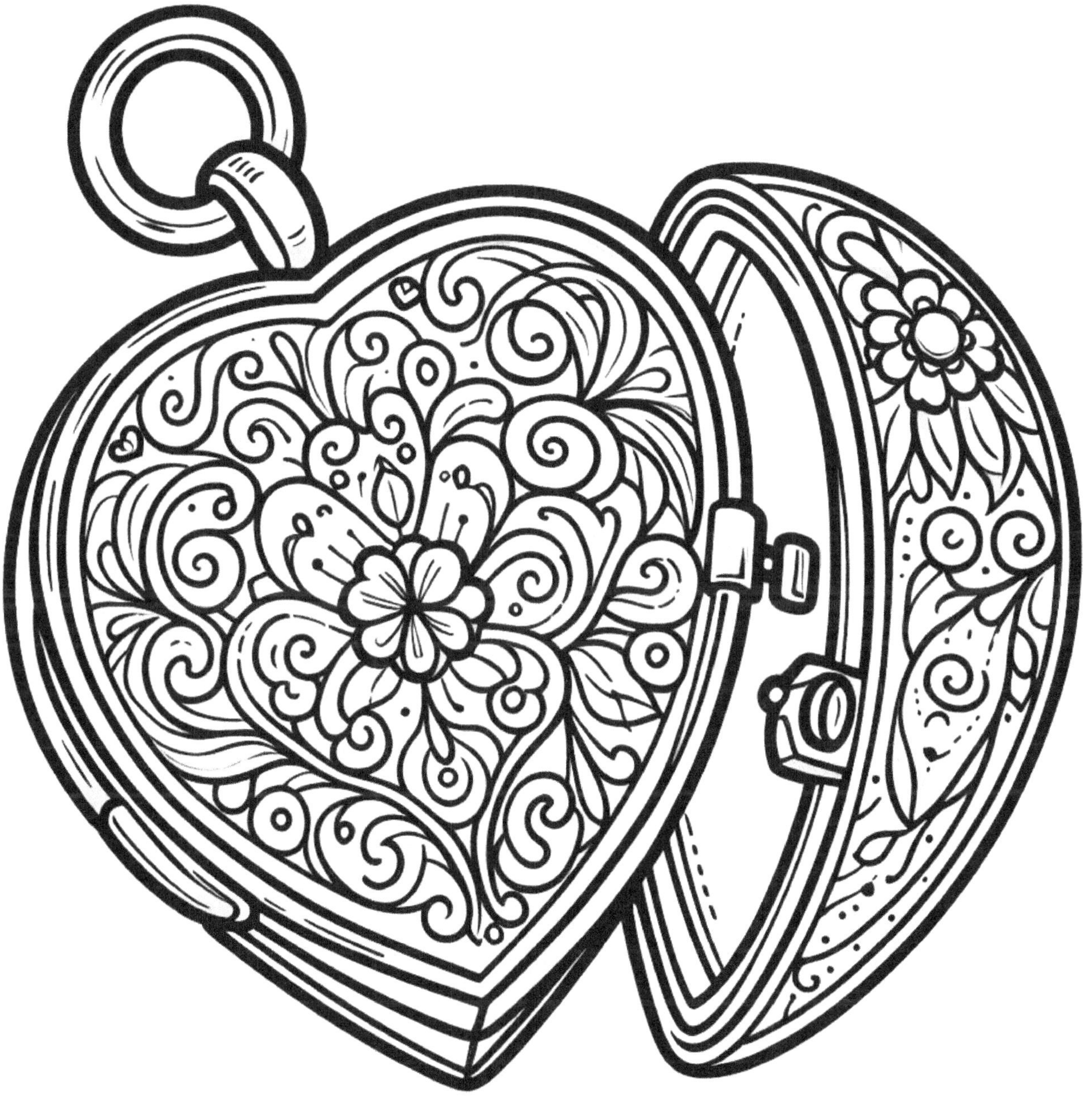

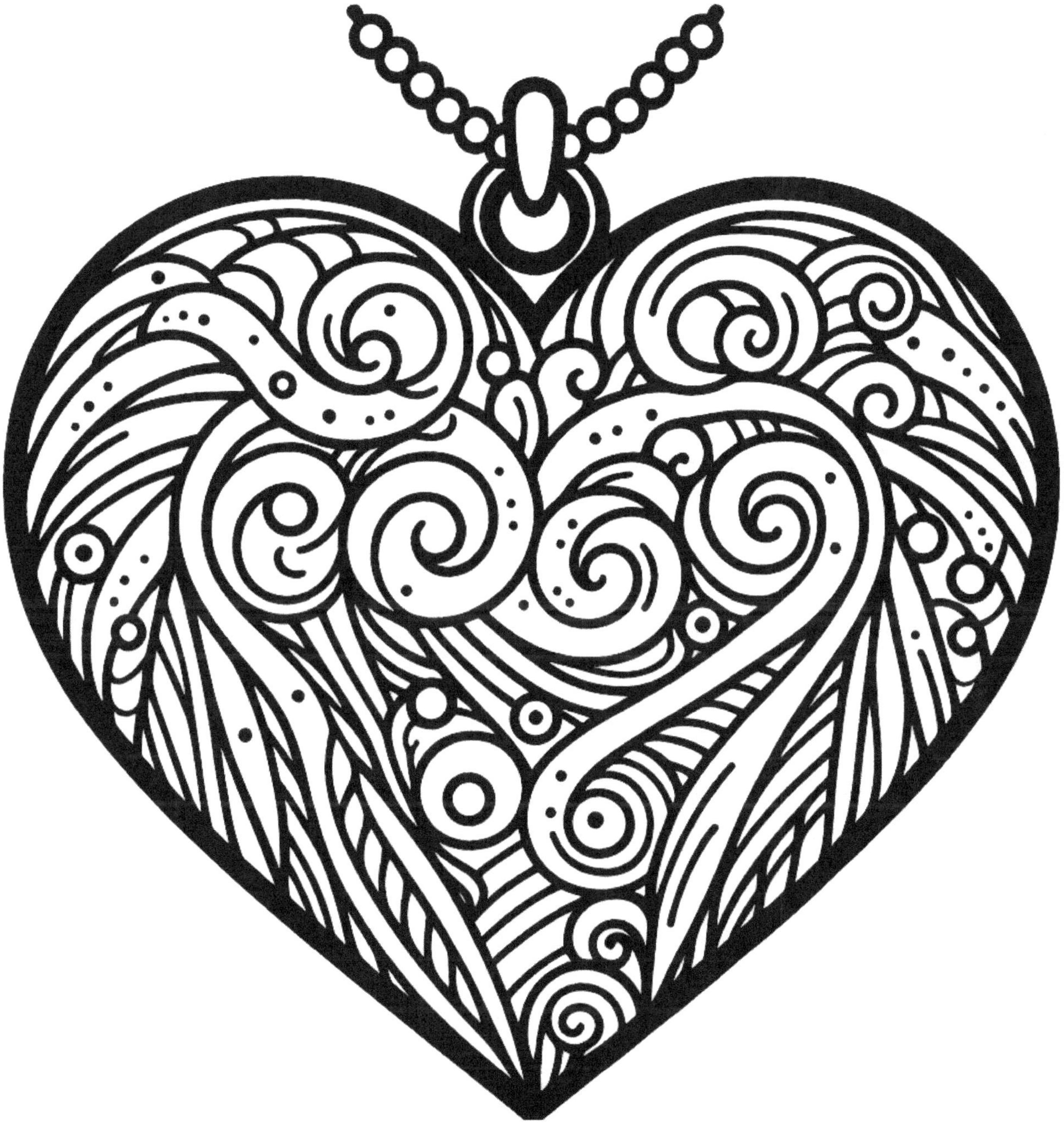

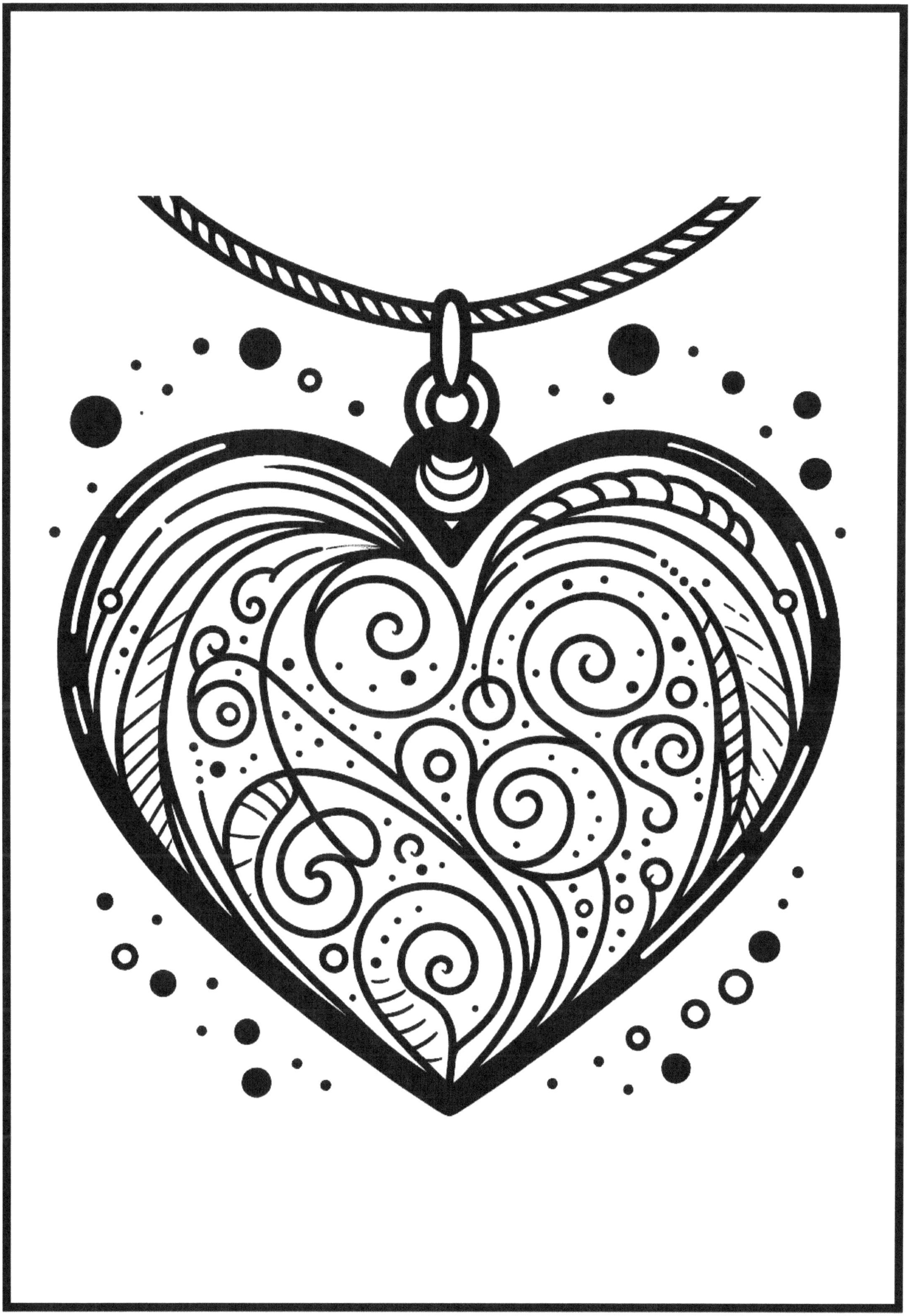

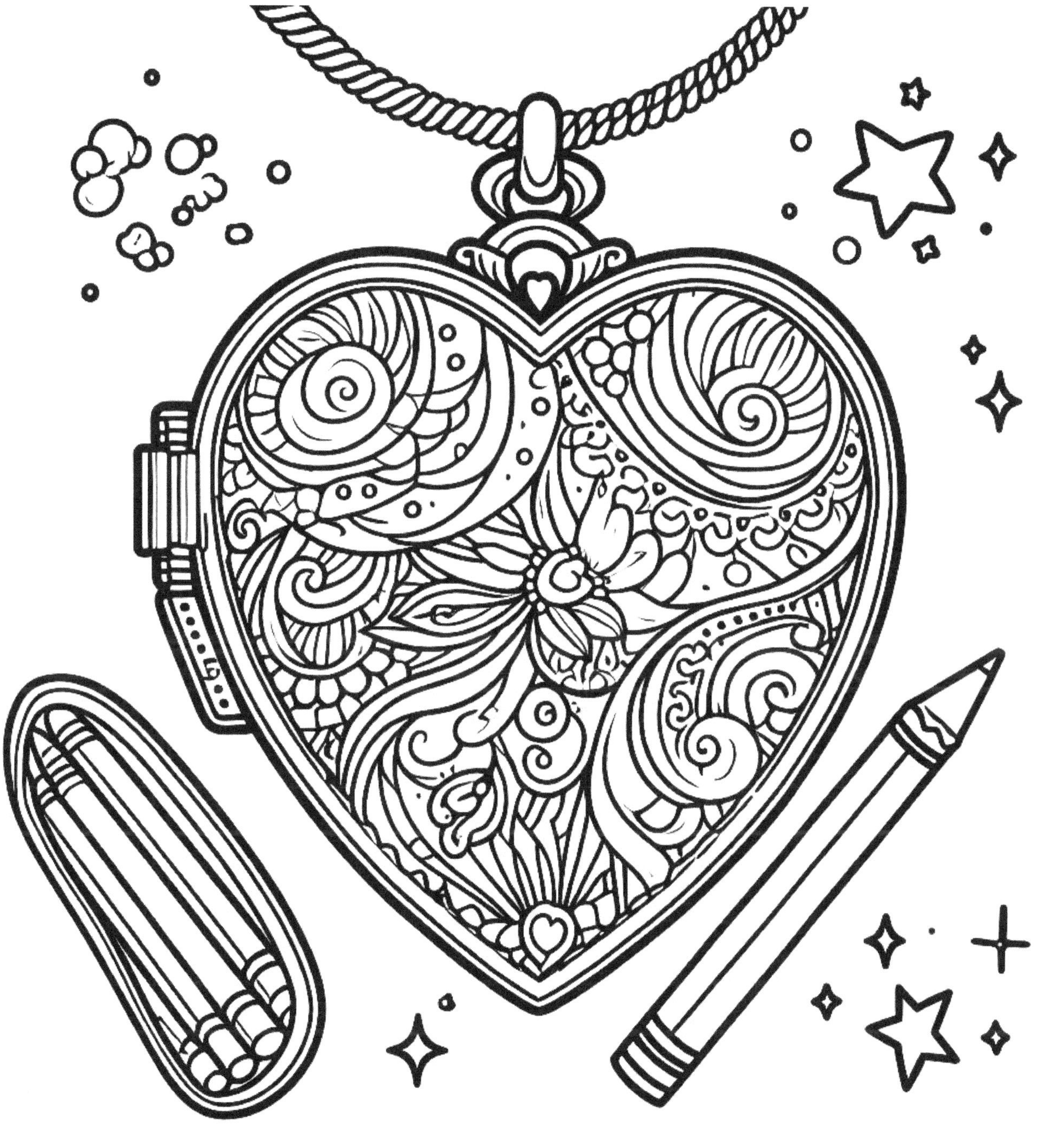

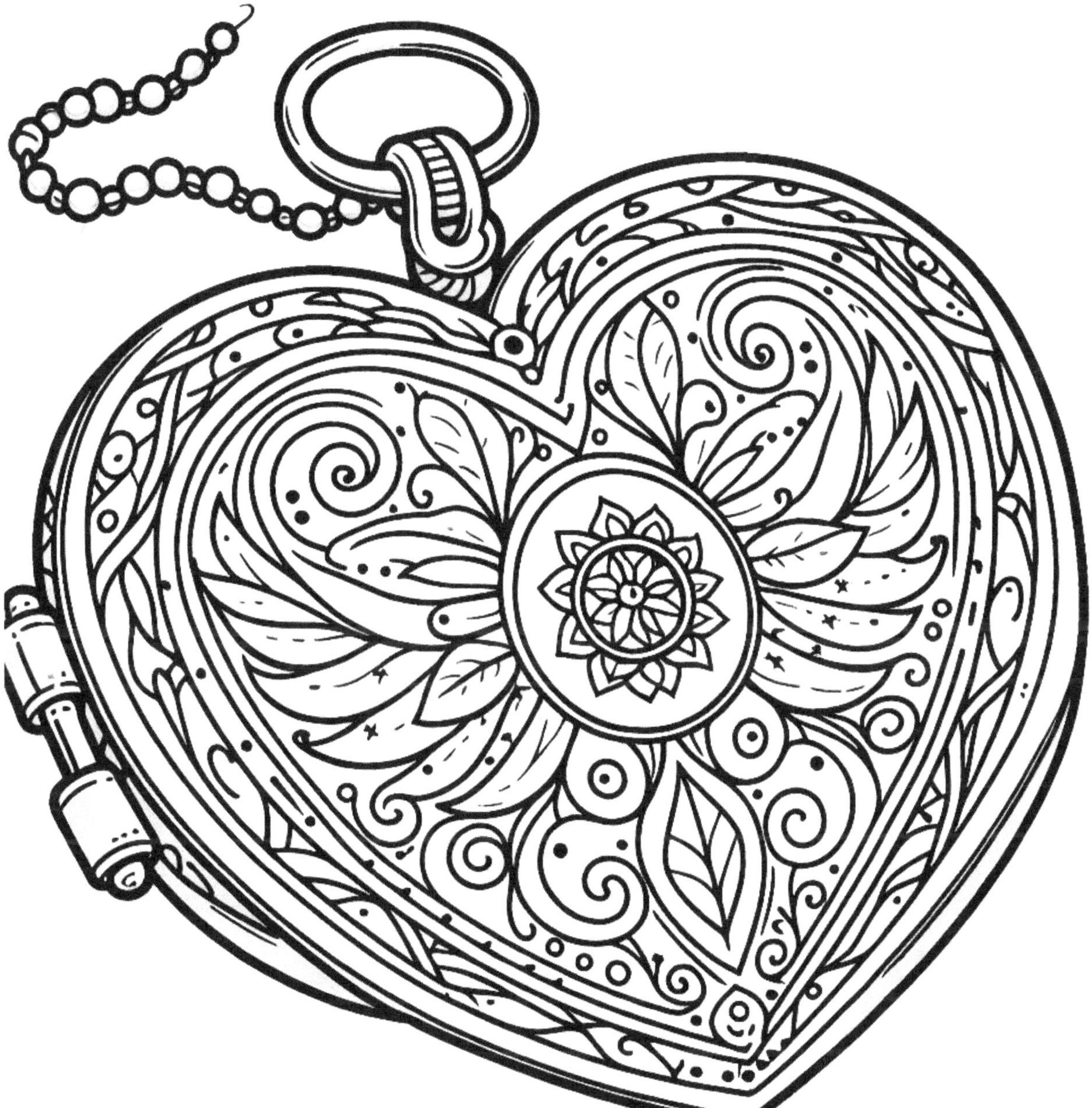

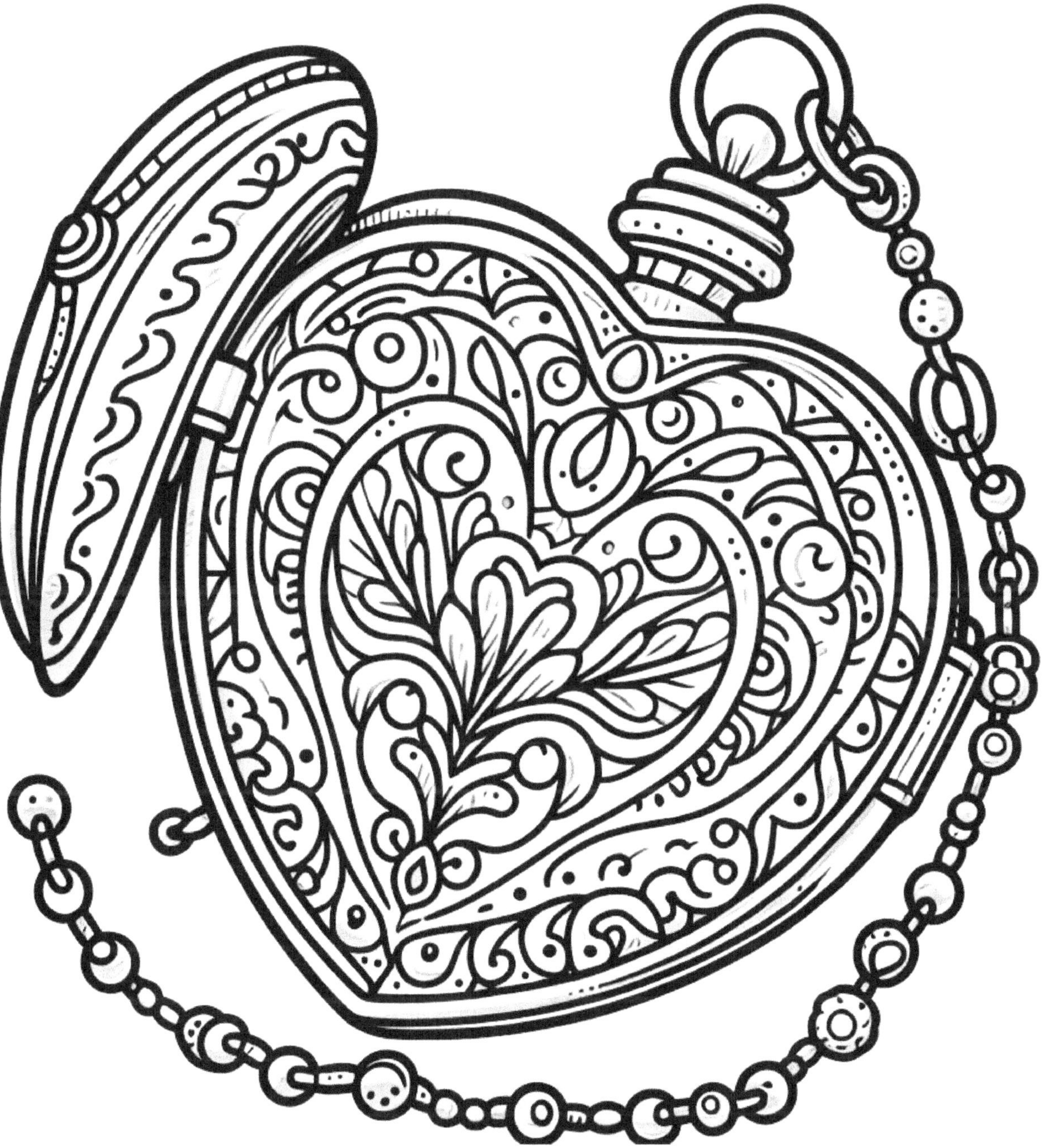

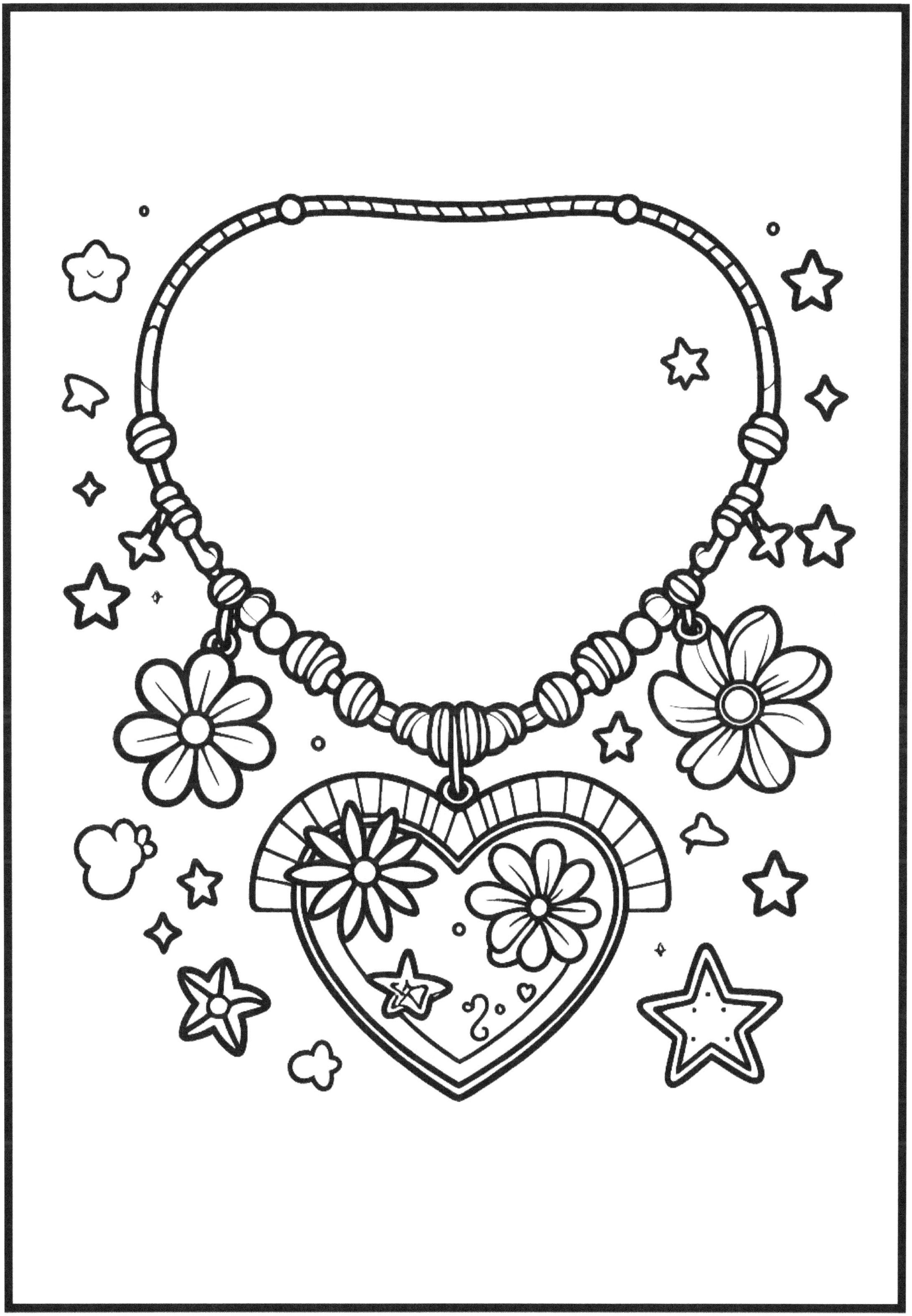

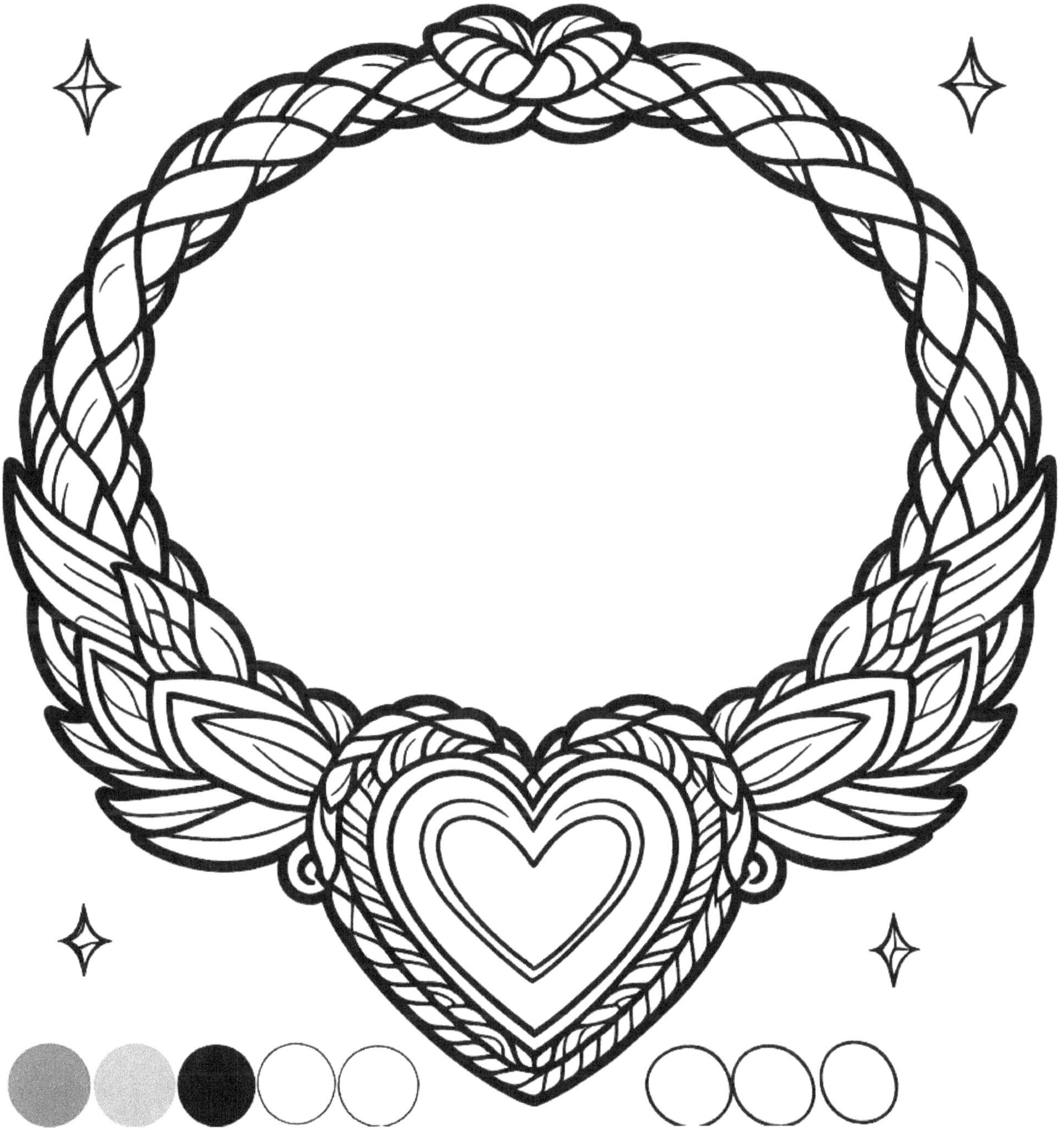

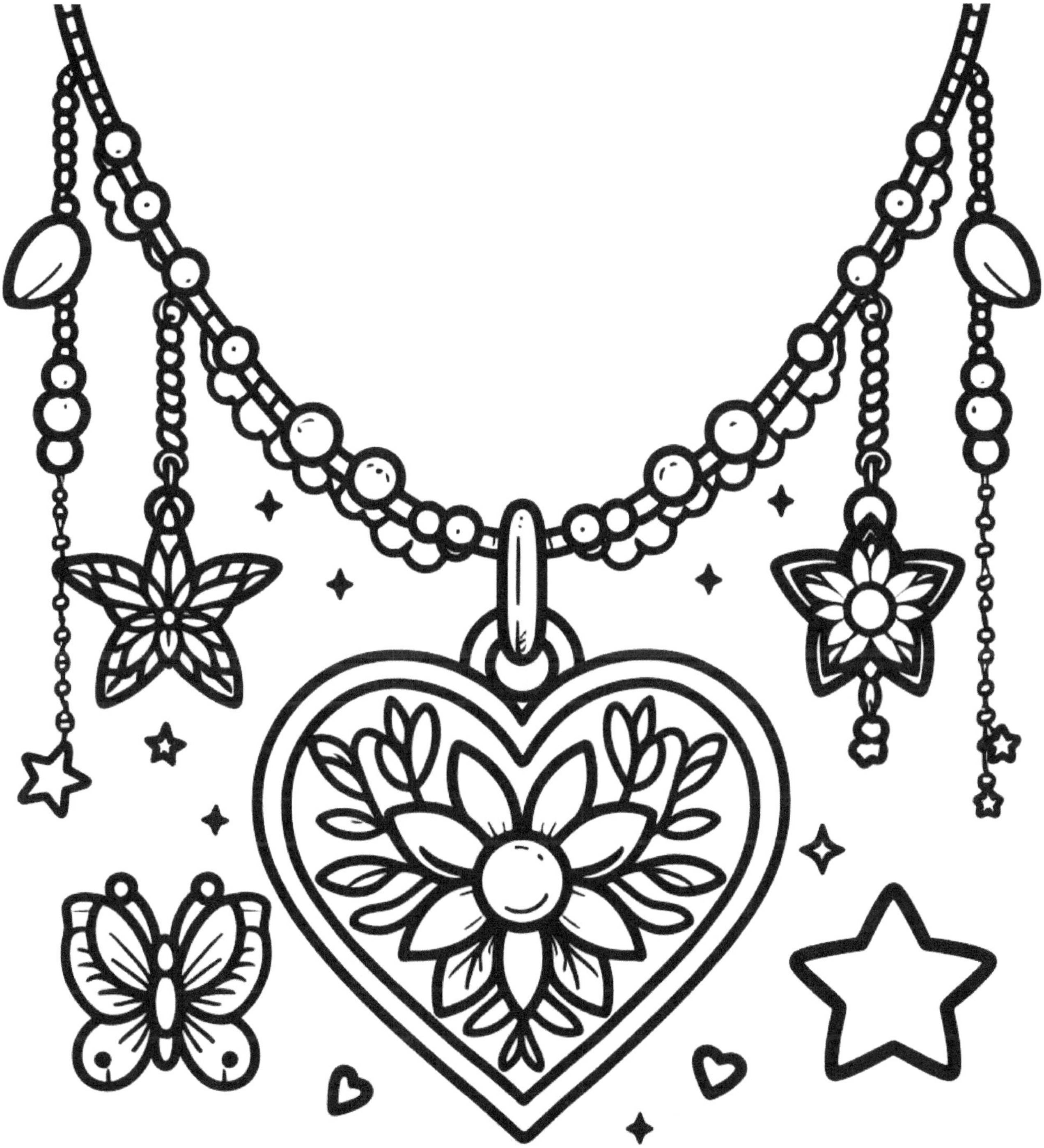

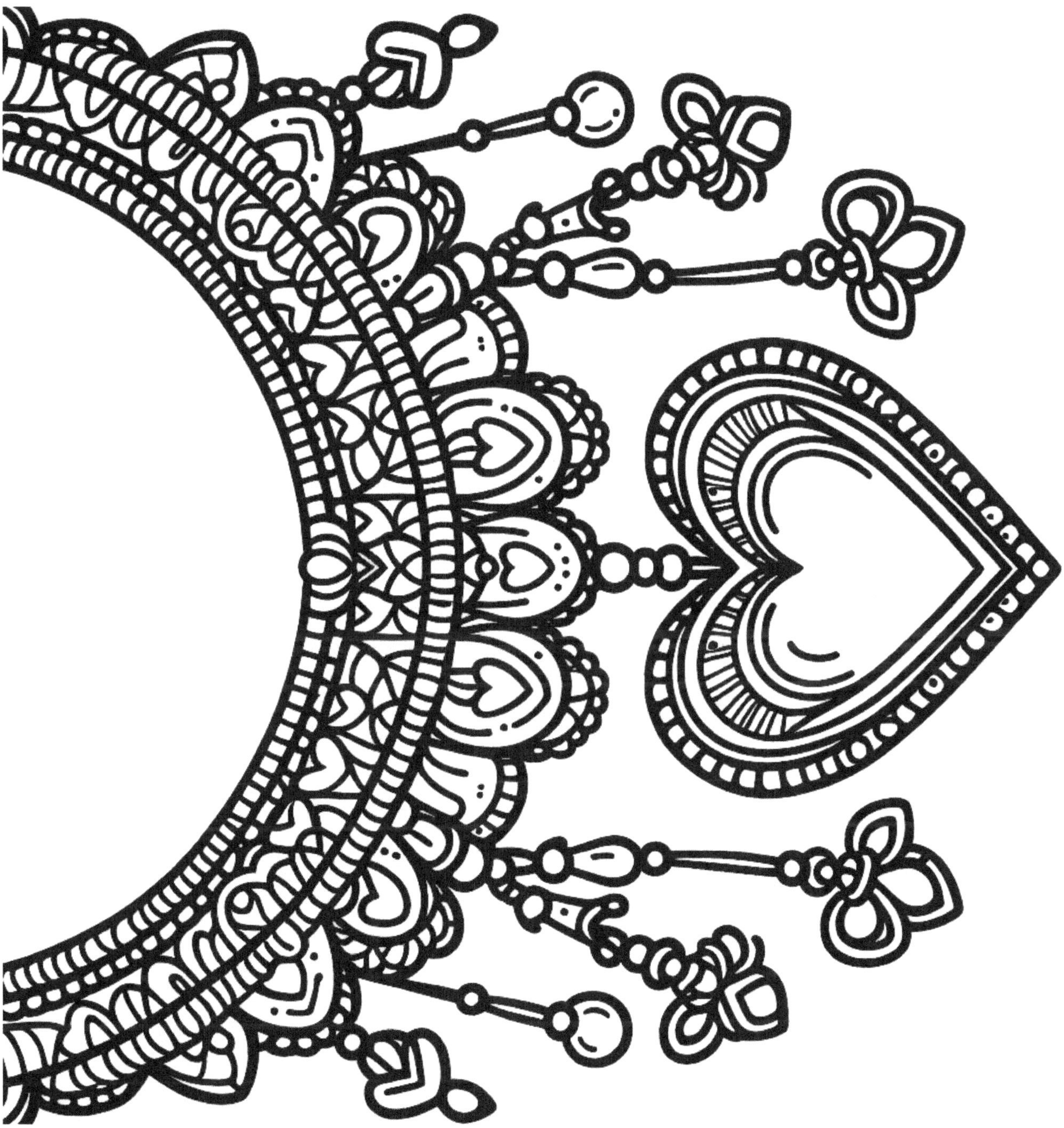

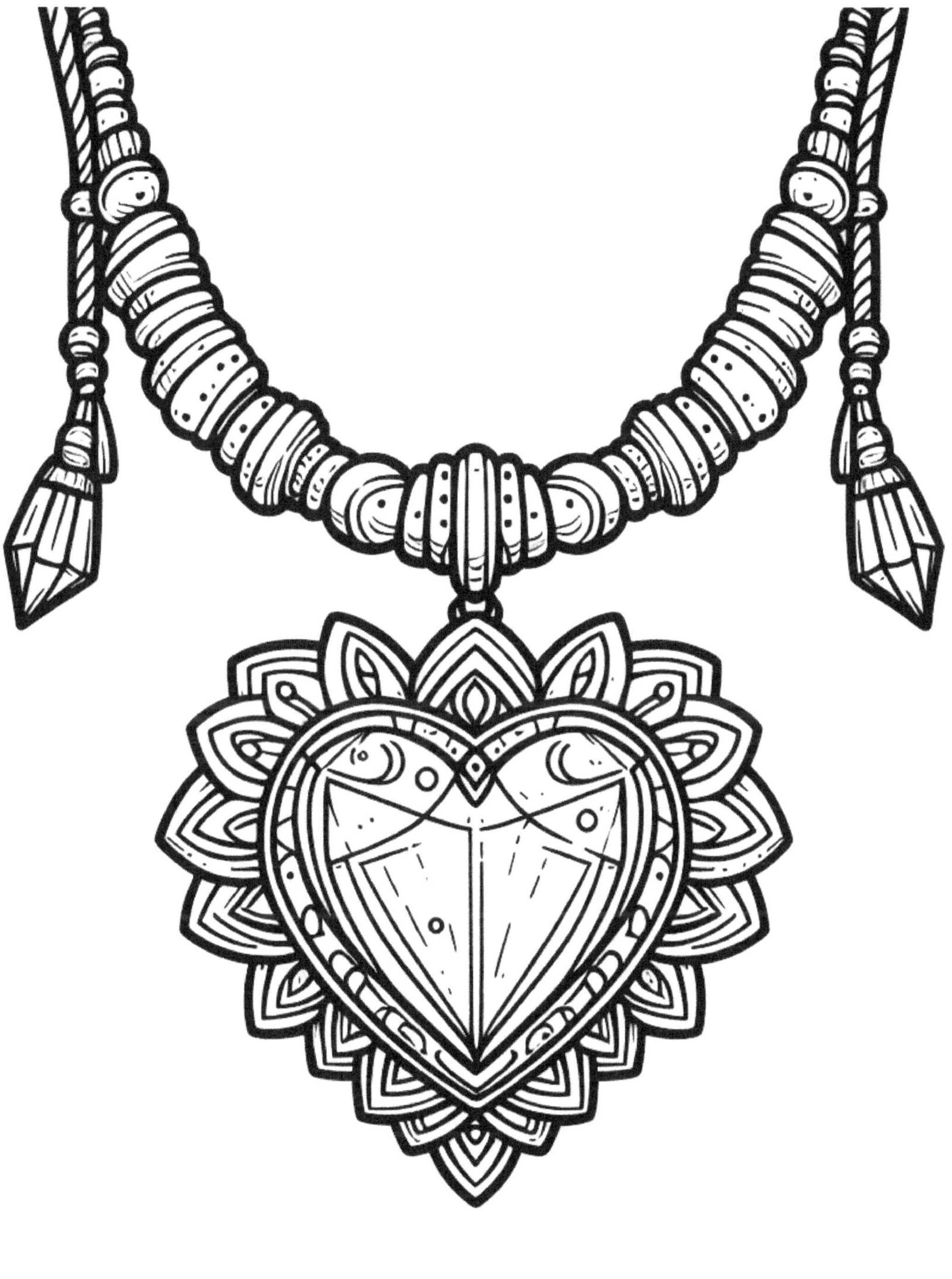

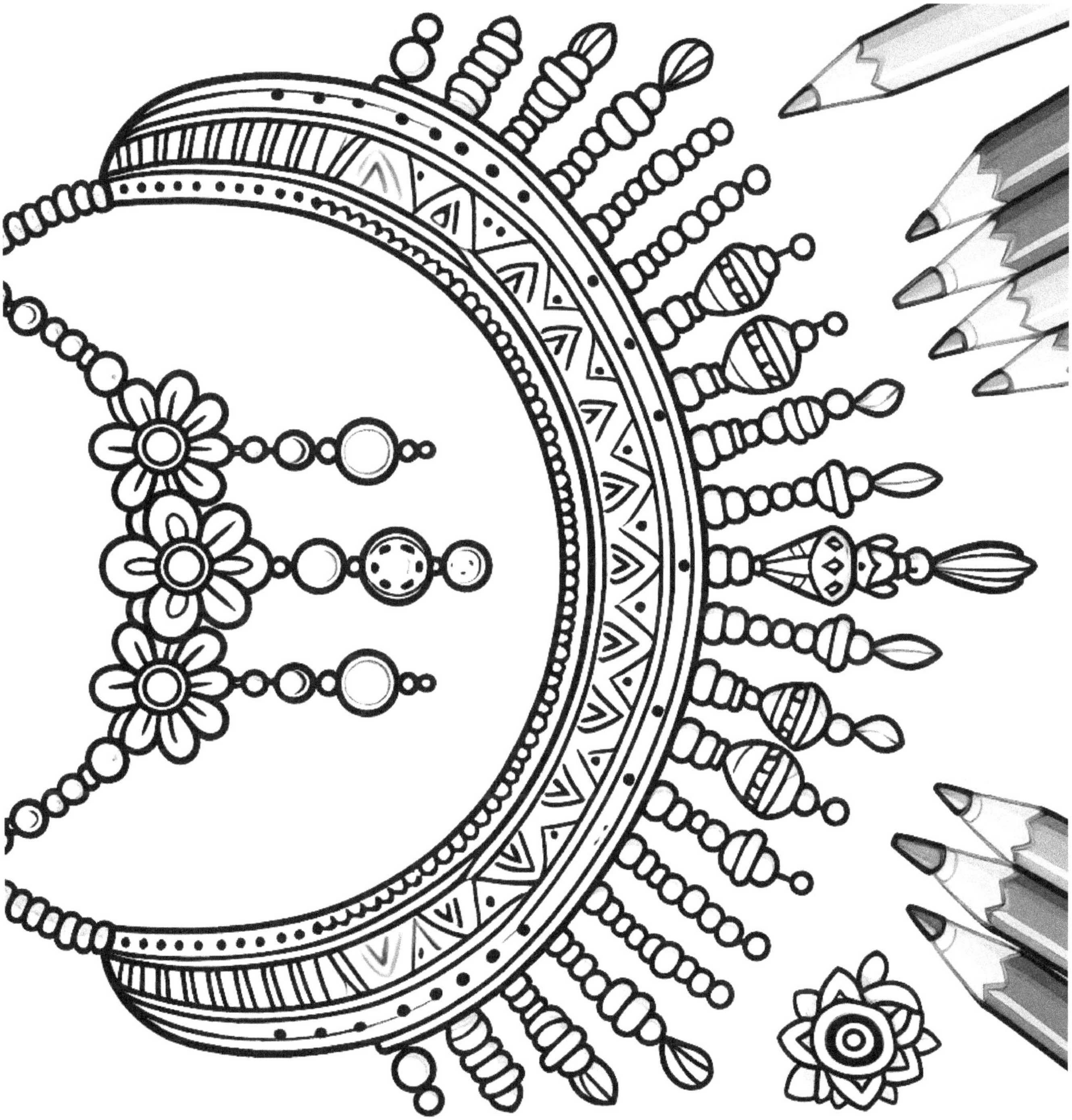

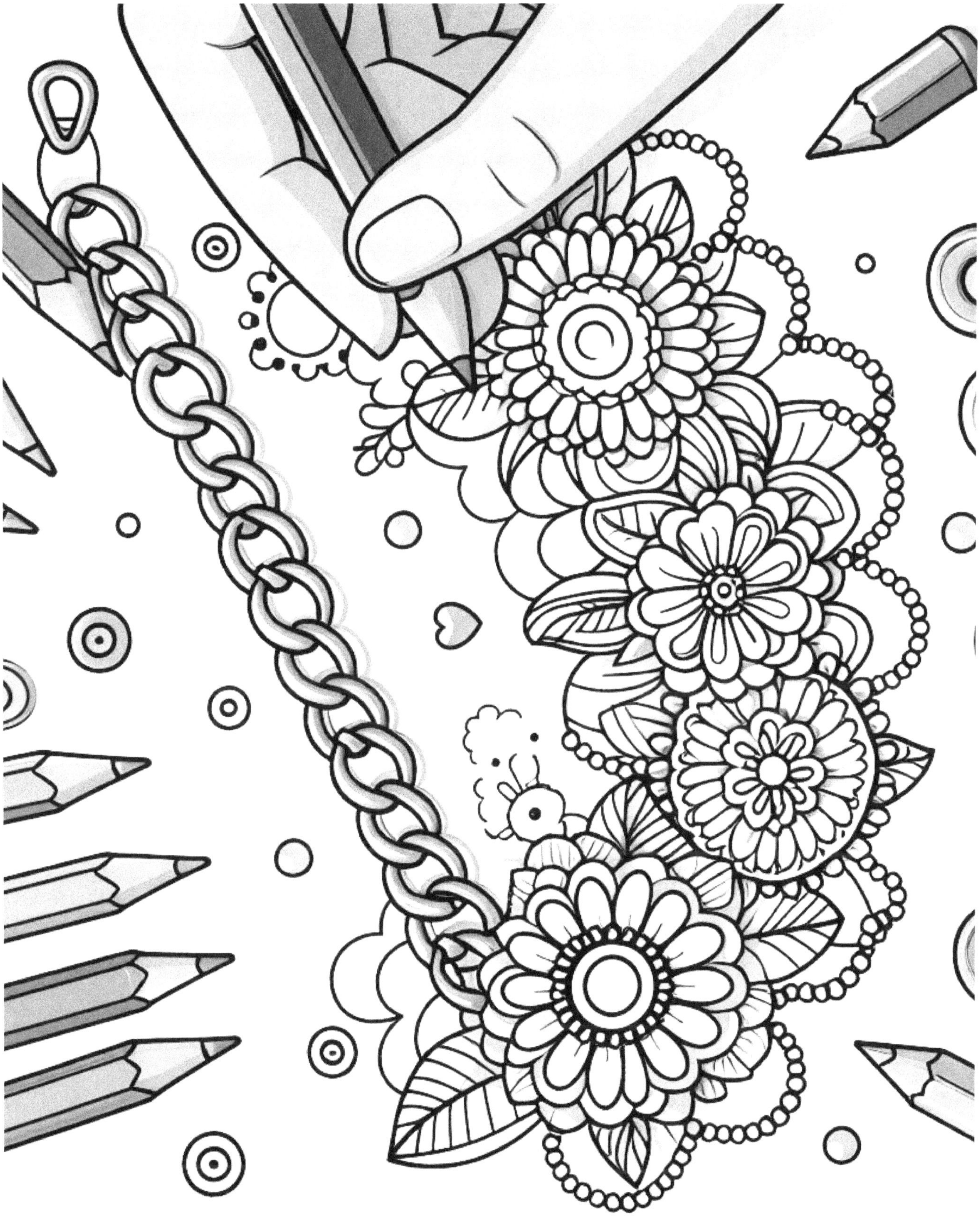

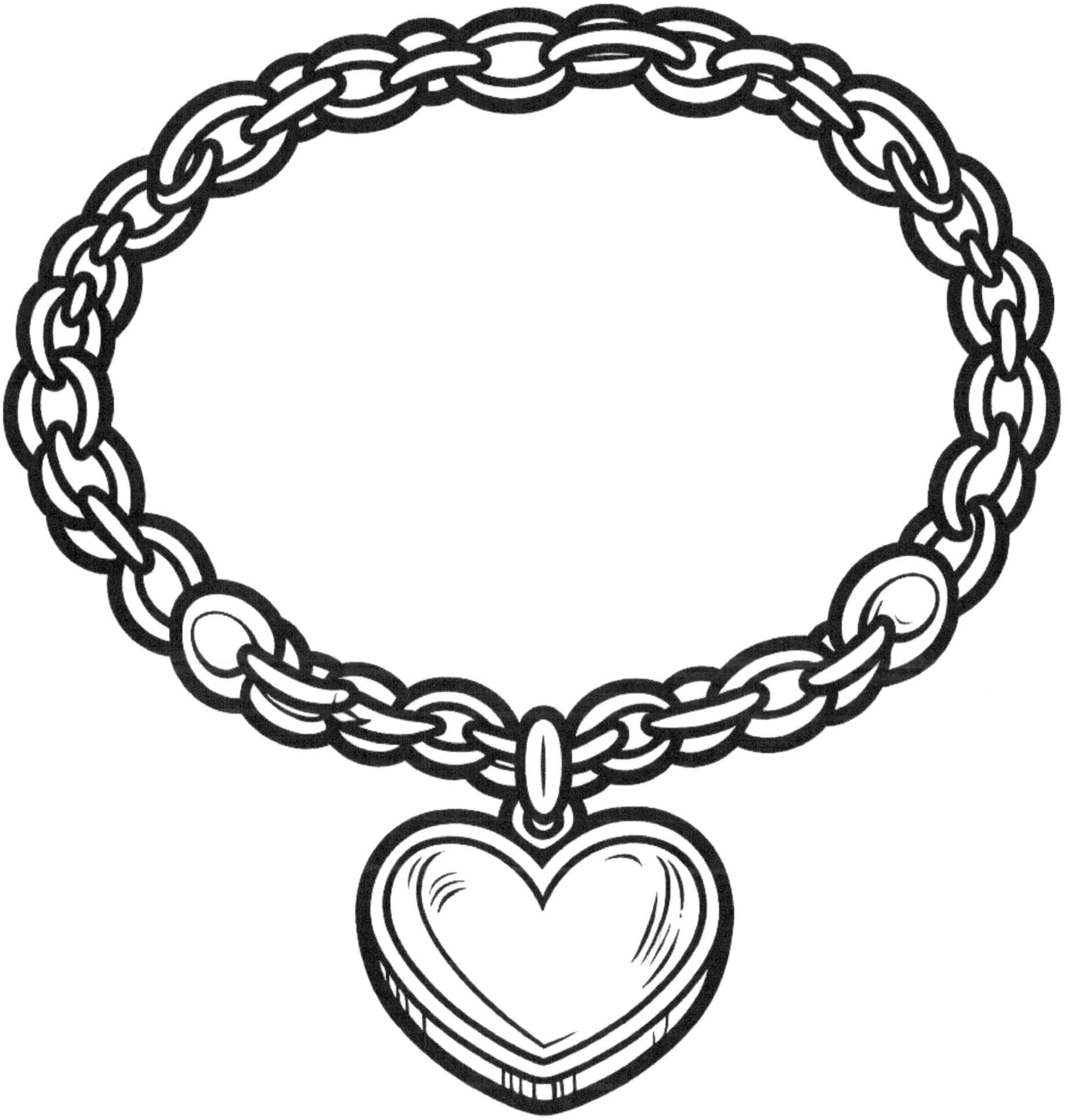

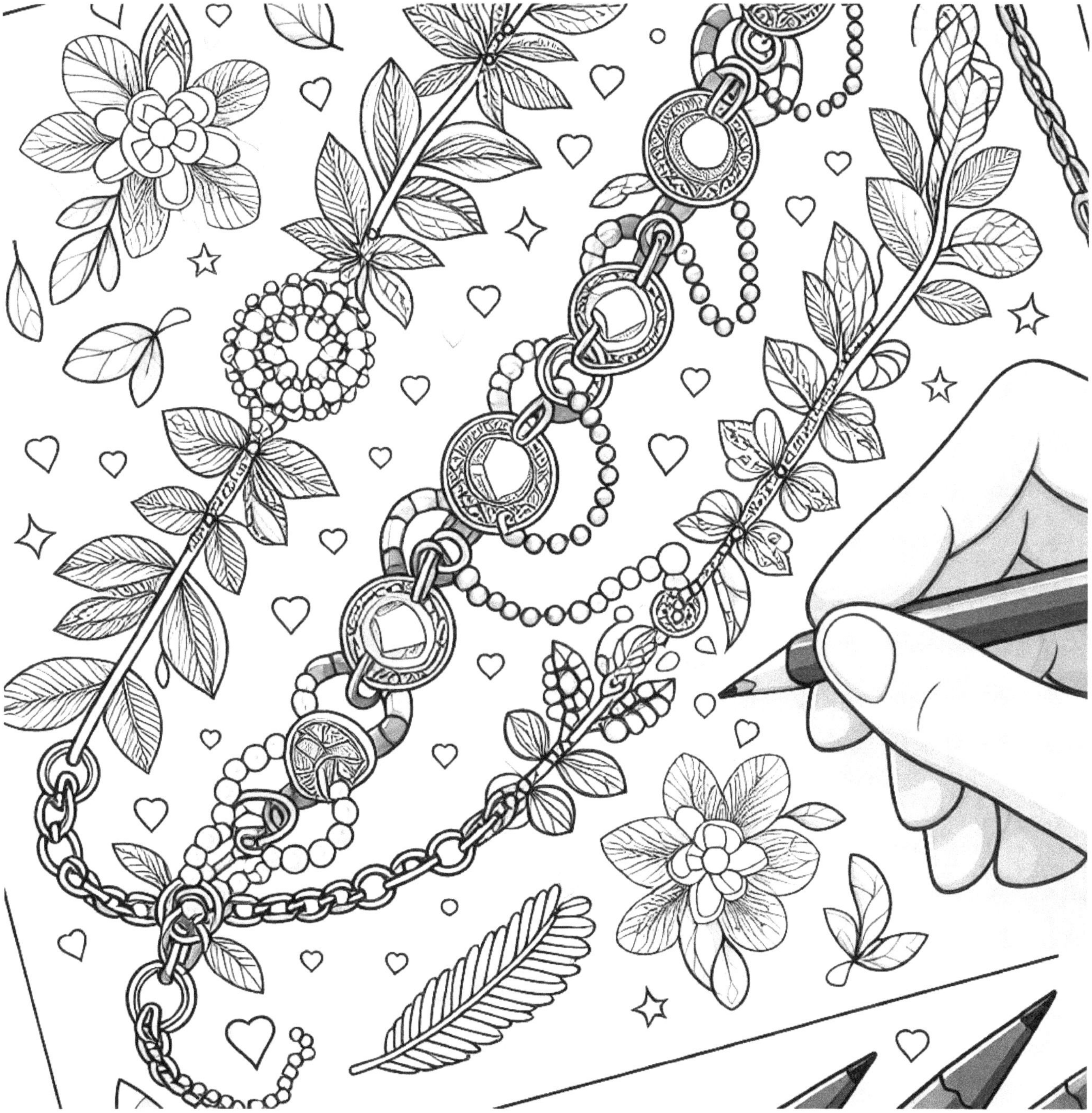

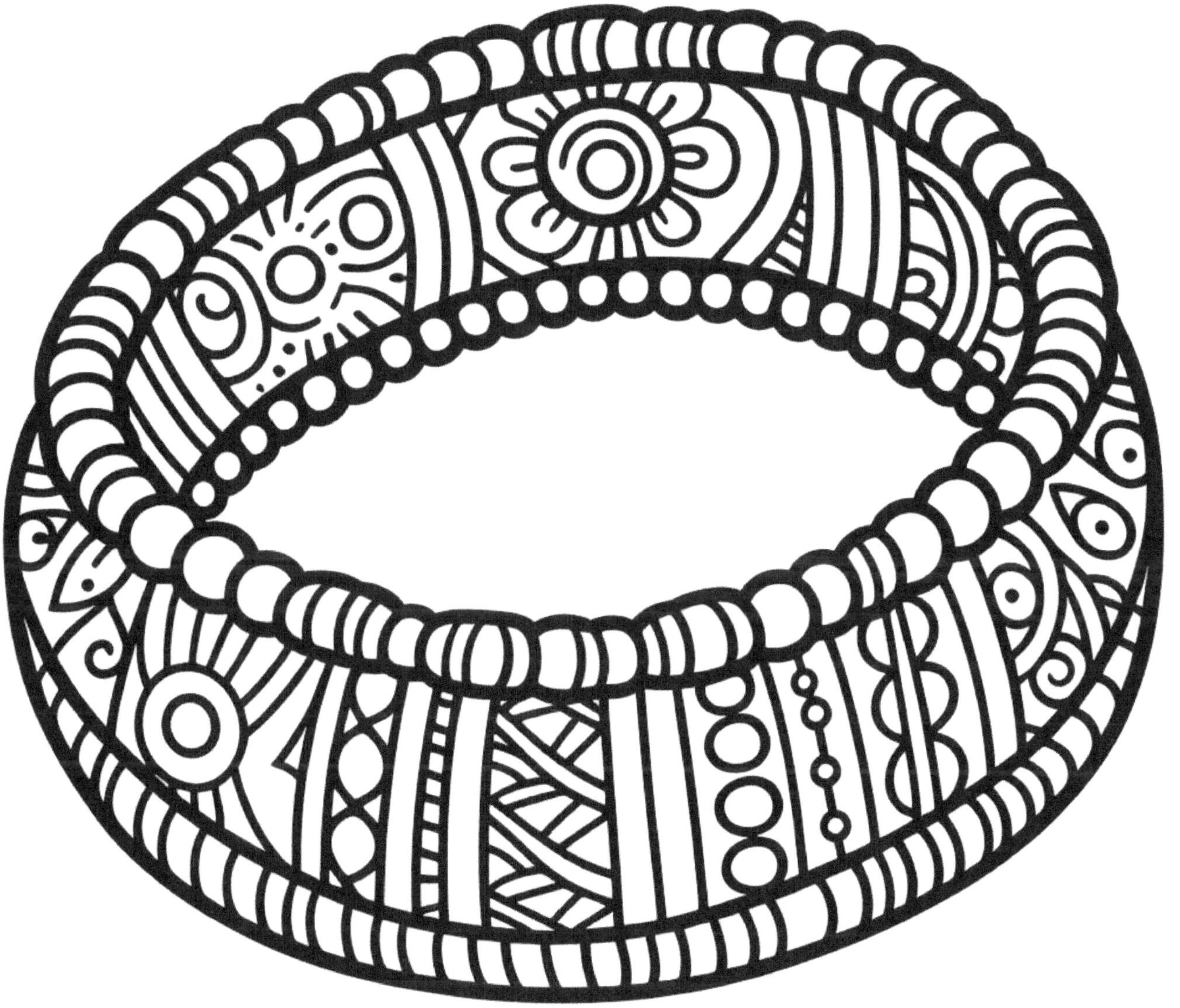

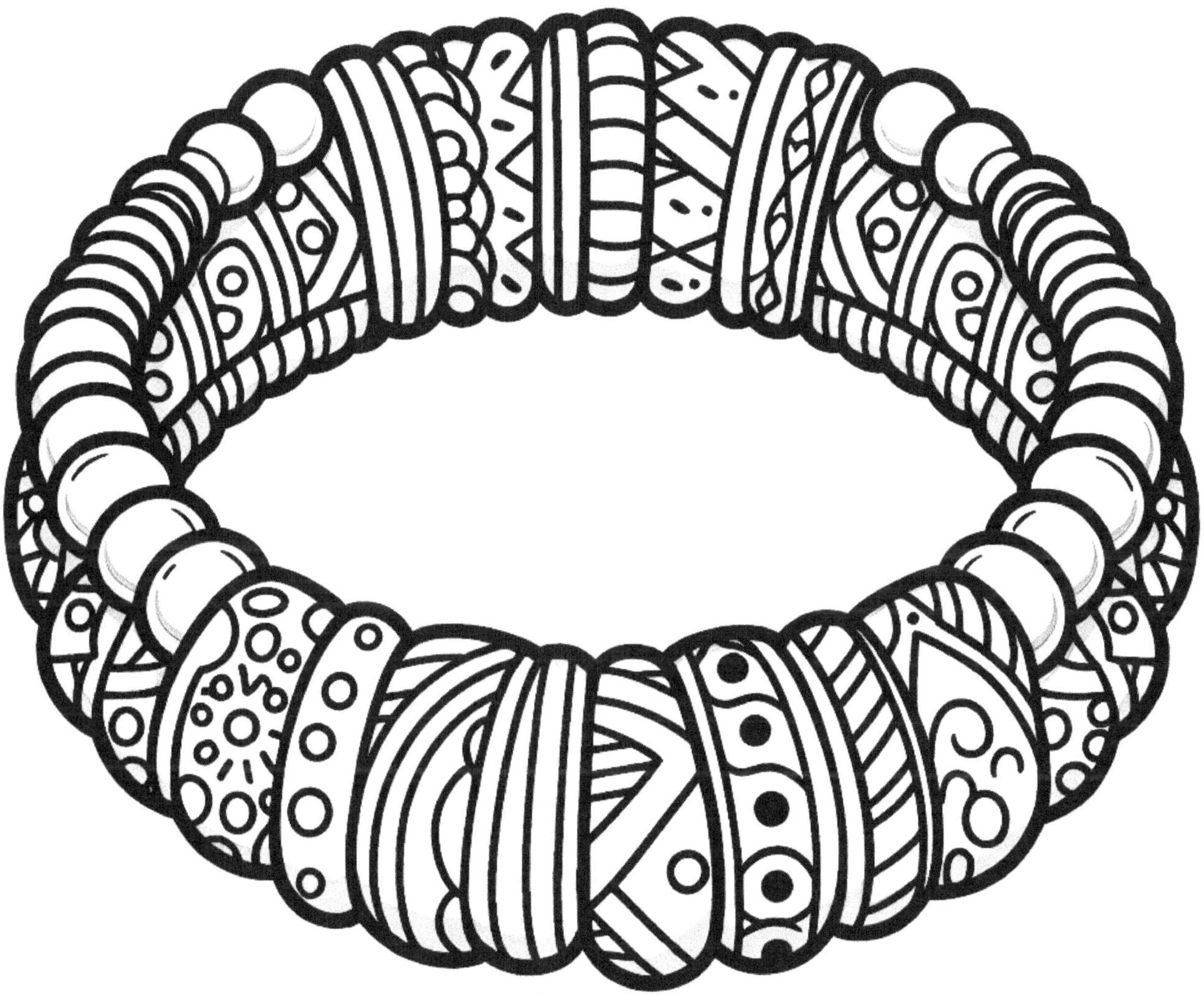

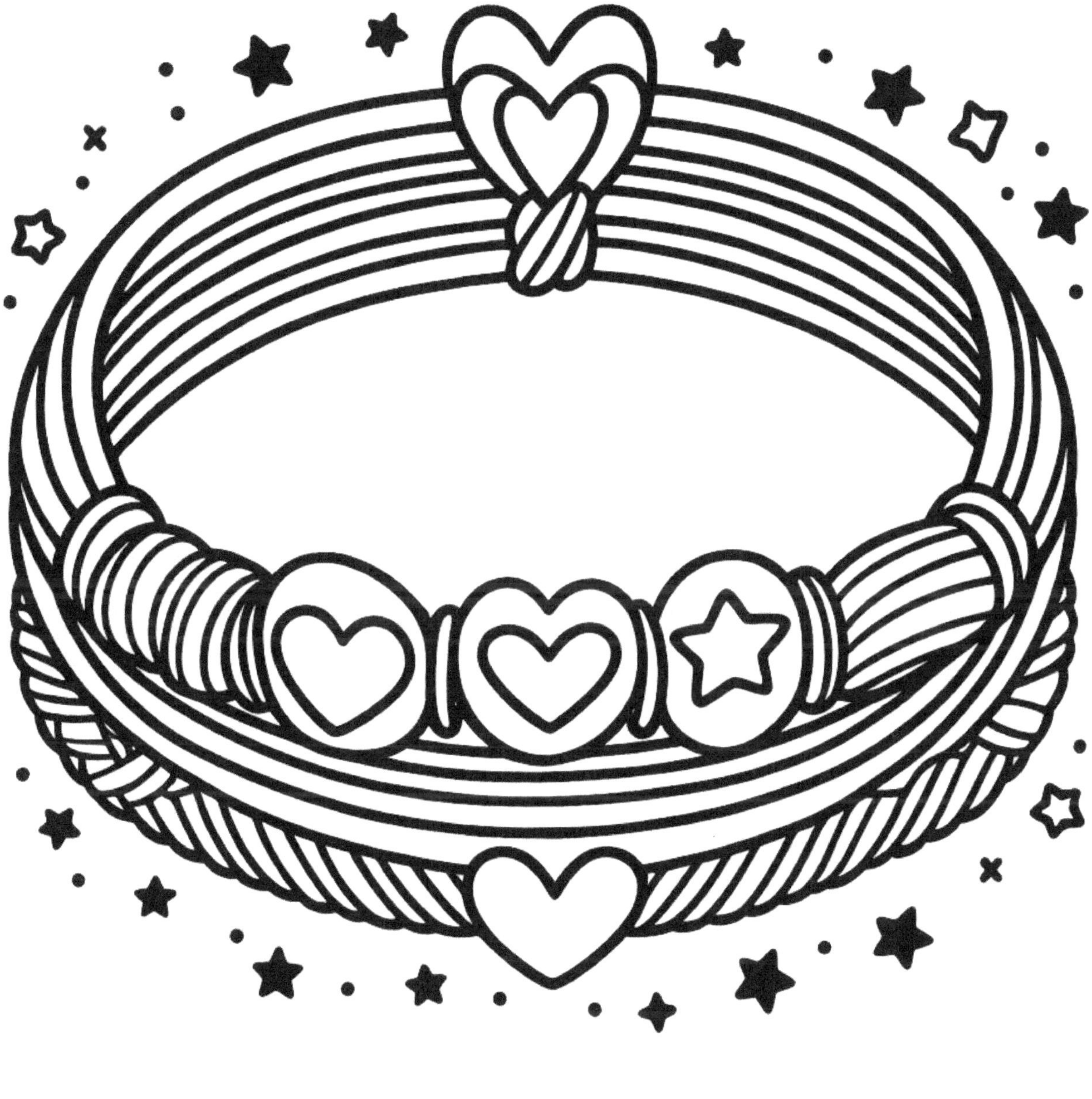

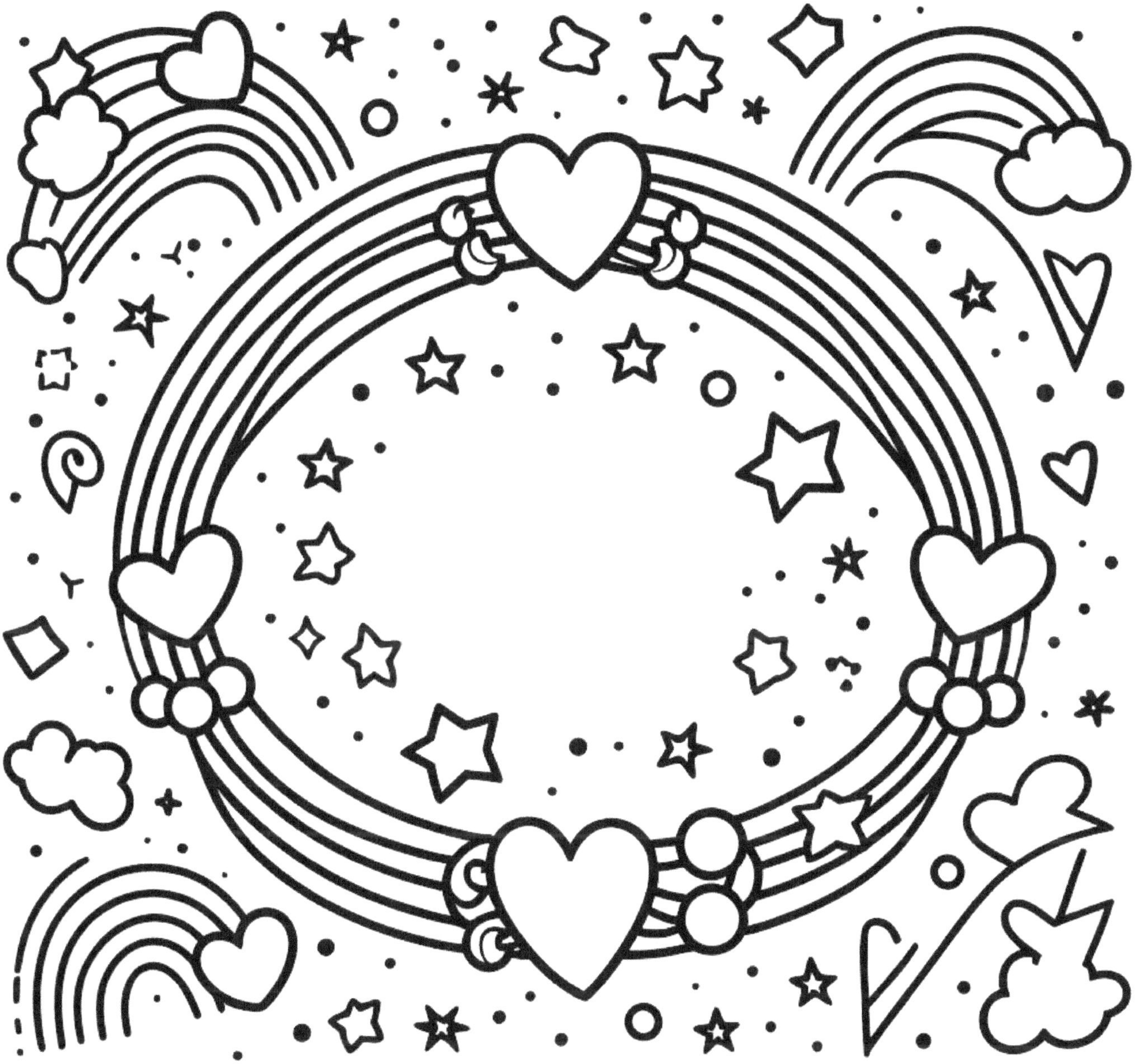

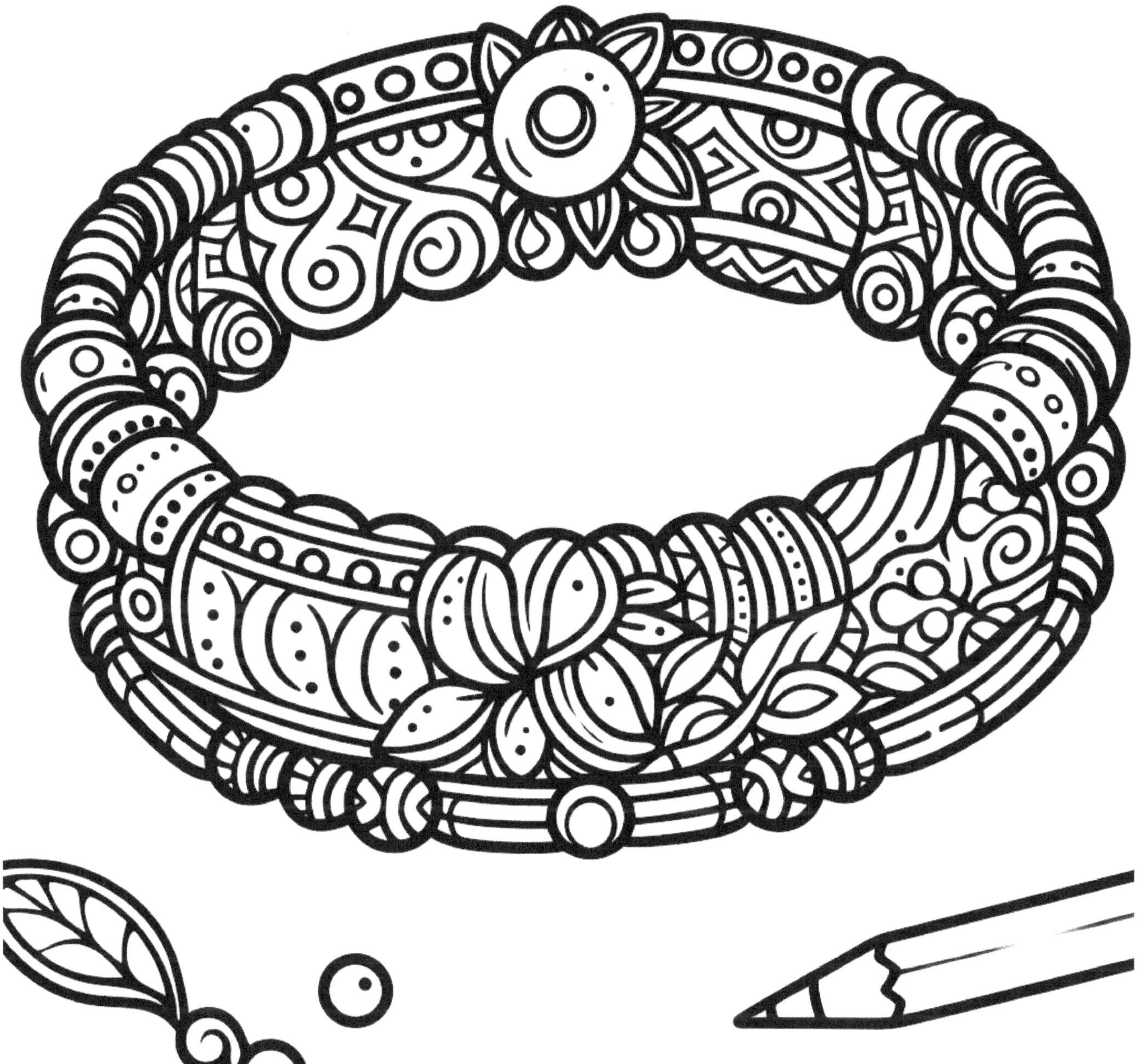

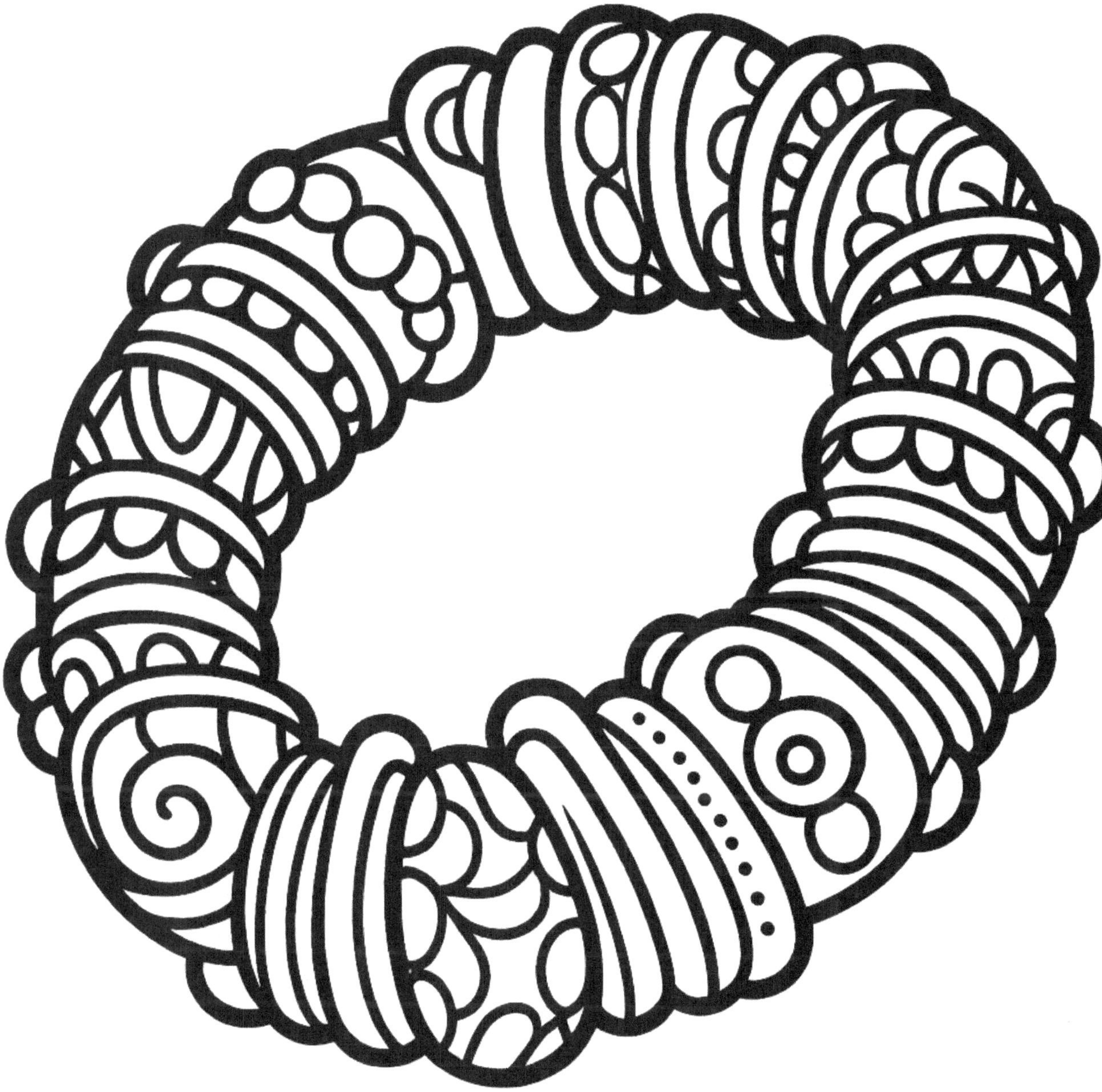

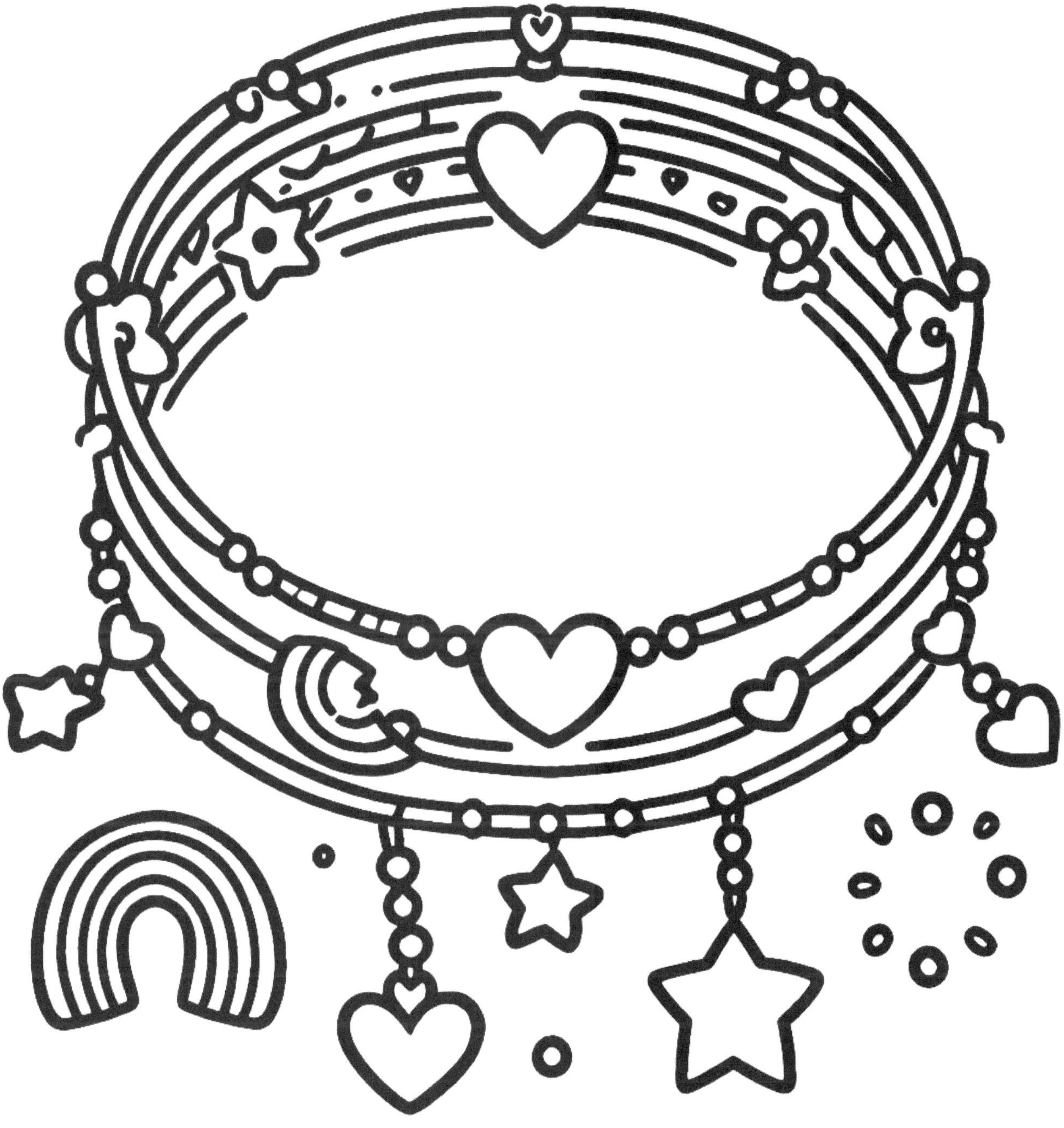

www.ingramcontent.com/pod-product-compliance
Lightning Source LLC
Chambersburg PA
CBHW062311220526
45470CB00013B/3174
9798325162039